SPRING CLEAN YOUR PLANET!

Also in Beaver by Ralph Levinson
How To Turn Water Upside Down

With Paul Temple
How to Make Square Eggs

SPRING CLEAN YOUR PLANET!

Investigate pollution with these exciting experiments!

Ralph Levinson

Illustrated by Sally Kindberg
Foreword by Richard Branson

Beaver Books

A Beaver Book
Published by Arrow Books Limited
62–5 Chandos Place, London WC2N 4NW
An imprint of Century Hutchinson Ltd

London Melbourne Sydney Auckland
Johannesburg and agencies throughout the world

First published 1987

Text © Ralph Levinson 1987
Illustrations © Century Hutchinson Ltd 1987

This book is sold subject to the condition that it shall not, by way of trade or otherwise, be lent, resold, hired out, or otherwise circulated without the publisher's prior consent in any form of binding or cover other than that in which it is published and without a similar condition including this condition being imposed on the subsequent purchaser.

Set in Century Schoolbook
by JH Graphics Ltd, Reading

Made and printed in Great Britain
by Anchor Brendon Ltd
Tiptree, Essex

ISBN 09 947230 9

Contents

Foreword	6
Introduction	7
Litter Blitz	9
Acids Are Innocent, OK?	45
Are Habitats Habitable?	76
The Painful Lesson of Nuclear Energy	104
Fact File	117
Action!	120

Foreword

Hello, I'm Richard Branson. You've probably seen me on the telly. But you may not know that I'm in charge of a very important new campaign – UK 2000 – which most people call 'Clean up Britain'.

Pollution today is a very serious problem. Yet we think of it as something we have to put up with. Like rice pudding. Or spiders in the bath. It takes a terrible disaster like the accident at Chernobyl to make us stand up and shout about it. That's why I wholeheartedly recommend this book.

Spring Clean Your Planet tells you all about pollution through easy and fun to do projects. It then suggests ways you can help. Like telling your friends to stop chucking their chip papers around. And forming or joining societies to try and stop factories causing pollution. You'd be surprised at just how much you can do! So go ahead – read on!

Introduction

So you want to spring clean your planet? You'll need a bionic broom to help you. Dip your mop in the oceans and the Earth will be as clean as a whistle in no time at all. Mission possible? Yes. You won't do it in one day but you *can* make a start. It's all up to you, and the more people you can influence to help you spring clean our planet the quicker the job will be done.

The best place to begin is with a little bit of the planet – the place where you live. If that needs seeing to it's no good going elsewhere. Nowadays many things are damaging the health of our planet. There's litter, acid rain, radioactivity, needless waste, pesticides, lead pollution and much besides. In this book, we tackle the problems of acid rain, waste, nuclear power and the health of waterlife and trees. There are lots of experiments and projects you can do. You can investigate your area and have fun at the same time. At the back of the book there's advice on how to start your own action group and a list of organizations that will help you. There is also a book list.

You have to become a detective in your attempt to find out what is killing off the plant and animal life around us. Keep a notebook and pencil handy to gather any evidence you may come across. If you have a camera it will help to take photographs of areas you investigate. As a scientist, you are going to use science to work out many of your results. As a journalist, you are going to bring anything that's wrong to people's attention. And as a really *good* politician, you are going to work with your friends to make your surroundings better.

And now it's time to give that broom an airing...

Star Rating

The number of stars by each project is a guide to its difficulty

*   Simple
* * Straightforward but time-consuming
* * * Time-consuming and challenging. Needs help of an adult or teacher

Litter Blitz

Some people have strange ideas about improving the area where they live. They cover paving stones and grass verges with oily chip papers, cigarette papers, lollipop papers, chocolate papers, toffee papers, newspapers, sticky papers, crisp packets, food wrappings, old cardboard boxes and magazine covers. Others decorate our parks and gardens with them. No wonder you often find a newspaper folding itself around your feet on a windy day or even flying in your face. And it's not surprising householders get rather bored of sweeping all the papers away.

Then there are the real litter bugs. They don't stop at papers and plastics. No. They contribute orange peel, drink cans and bottles − and often the cans have sharp edges or the bottles are broken so nasty accidents happen. But we must not forget the banana skin specialists. What a boring life it would be without those slippery people!

Well, it seems that a lot of odd people think like that. You can see them on any street dropping papers as they walk along, throwing things out of car windows and tossing rubbish into other people's homes. We have a real litter problem and it won't go away by itself. We have to do something about it. In this chapter you will find lots of fascinating facts about rubbish, yes rubbish, and ways you can stop the litterbug headache. Did you know you can make music from rubbish? Or make money out of waste?

Or grow plants in refuse? The fun's about to start. Read on . . .

Roman Litterbugs

Fortunately, the Romans were real wastrels. They left their litter all over the place. Their refuse tells us volumes about the way they lived. We know about the clothes they wore, the coins they exchanged and the pots and pans they used. Archaeologists and scientists have sifted through all the rubbish and reconstructed the way of life of the Romans.

If you think you're doing future archaeologists a favour by leaving litter around, think again. We can record our history in so many ways — books, newspapers, film, photographs, sound and video-recordings, micro-film, computer data banks — that any claim that there is a good reason for leaving litter lying around can only be described as a load of old rubbish.

What's In The Bin?

Do you think waste is just a load of old rubbish? Take a closer look at the stuff in your dustbin. Stop! Don't empty it on the best carpet. This is what you would find in the average dustbin:

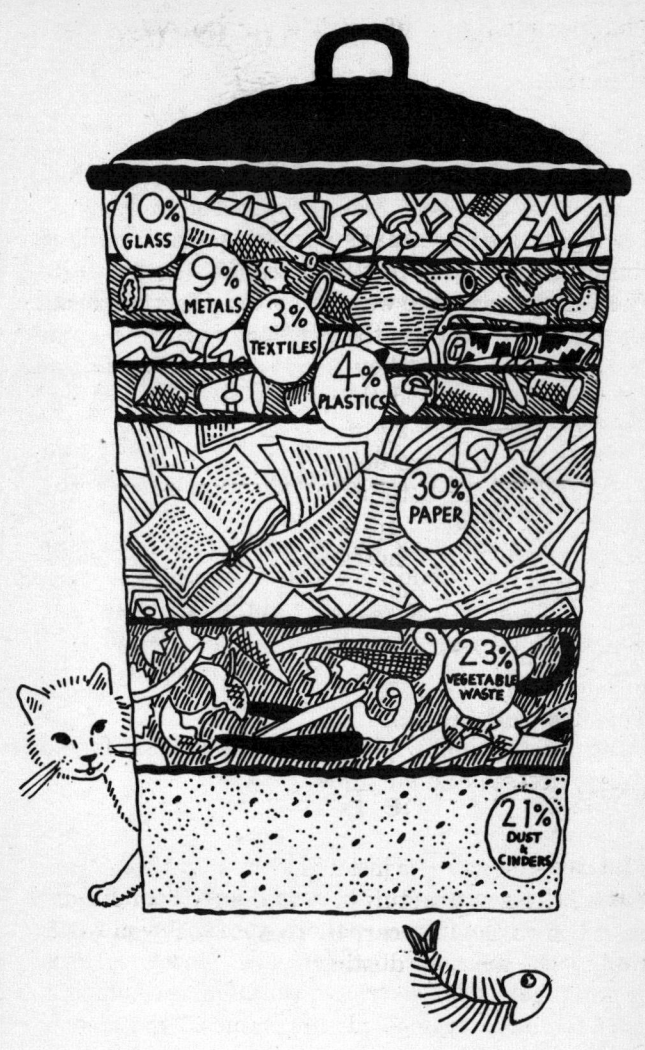

Don't Waste Waste Or Refuse Refuse

Glass
Fact: Making glass consumes so much energy that milk bottles have been redesigned to a stumpy shape. Six old bottles were made from the same amount of glass that can now make ten stumpy bottles.
Fact: Glass waste makes sand paper, reflective paint, paving slabs, floor tiles and litter bins.

Metals and cans
Fact: If all the tin cans used each year in Britain were stacked end to end they would circle the Equator 40 times.
Fact: If you saved all the waste tin cans each year in Britain you would be worth £15 million.
Fact: Metals were so valuable in the last world war that old saucepans were used to make aeroplanes.

Textiles and fabrics
Fact: Dusters and wiping cloths are made from old shirts, dresses and curtains.

Plastics
Fact: Fifty years ago there would have been hardly any plastic waste because there were so few plastics. Now, most bags, spectacle frames, lenses, cutlery, packing materials, electrical insulation, car bumpers, pens, computer casings, picture frames, windscreens, saucepan handles, kettles, cups, raincoats, shoes, knitting needles and reading lamps are made from plastics.

Fact: Plastics should never be burned as household waste. The fumes from burning plastics are poisonous.

Paper and board
Fact: Each year we cut down a forest the size of Wales to provide all Britain's paper.
Fact: Fast-growing conifer trees, like the spruce and the pine, are planted to replace our slower-growing deciduous trees. A ready supply of paper? Yes, that's the good news. Now for the bad news: an average conifer supports 16 species of wildlife. The deciduous oak supports 284 species.

Vegetable waste
Fact: Rotting vegetables improve the health of the soil.
Fact: In many parts of the world vegetable waste is converted into fuel.

Dust and cinders
Fact: Running tracks and pathways are coated and compacted with ash, dust and cinders.

GLASS

If you cannot use them
- Give empty milk bottles back to the milk-man.
- Return soft-drink bottles to the shops.
- Return all other bottles to the local bottle bank.

> **ACTION! No Bottle Bank?**
> Write to the Cleansing Department of your local council asking for one. If you're not satisfied with their reply get in touch with your local councillor.

But some you can use
Jam, coffee and sweet jars are ideal for storage. Clean and dry them. They are ideal for storing dried food like rice and beans. Many jars have attractive shapes and, with a little decoration, would make lovely pen stands.

Working with glass
You will need glass cutters. If you don't have a pair, try your local glass merchant or hardware store. Always ask an adult to do glass cutting for you.

A Miniature Greenhouse

Why not make an unusual garden or plot of earth by growing tropical plants? You'll need a heat gatherer to provide the plants with the conditions they're used to. What better than a very large glass bottle like an empty wine bottle? Ask an adult to cut off the base of the bottle cleanly with the glass cutters.

Place the bottle over the plant. It acts as a heat sink. Your tropical plants will flourish! Try the local garden centre for advice about plants.

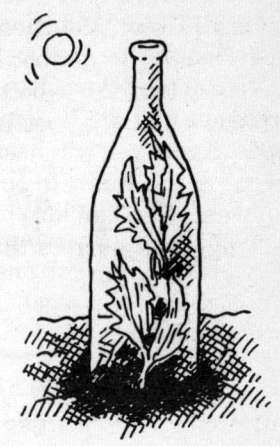

Flower Vases

Many spirit and wine bottles have such beautiful shapes that enthusiasts set up bottle collections. You'll need a lot of space for this. It's a pity to get rid of these bottles, so why not use them as flower vases? Many of the bottles are tinted in an attractive colour or you can paint the colourless bottles yourself.

Make Music!

With percussion instruments made from plastic bottles (see p. 19), and glass bottles, you're on your way to forming an unusual symphony orchestra, and making all sorts of different musical sounds.

You can use glass bottle instruments for percussion

or wind. Collect at least eight bottles of the same size and shape. Fill them with water to different heights. Tap each bottle with a spoon or a clean bone — what about all those lamb chops — and you will discover that each bottle produces a different note.

You can play the bottles in another way. Lick your forefinger and rub it quickly around the rim of each bottle. Again you will hear different notes. Adjust the height of the water in the bottle to obtain the note you want. You can also produce different sounds by blowing gently across the top of each bottle.

METALS AND CANS

Metals are money!
Empty aluminium drink cans are worth money. One can is worth about 1p. Organize proper can collections and you will earn yourself a lot of extra pocket money.

How do I know it's an aluminium can?
Tin cans contain iron. Aluminium cans don't, so they are non-magnetic. Hold a magnet against the side of the can. If the magnet doesn't stick then the can is made of aluminium. If you don't have a magnet, try the magnetic strip on the door of the refrigerator. Again, hold the side of the can against the door seal.

Where can I collect lots of cans?
Where lots of people buy soft drinks. Organize a team of friends with cardboard boxes and plastic sacks to collect the cans. The best places for waste cans are

stadiums, restaurants, cafés, clubs, stations, fairs and fêtes.

How can I store the cans?
Wash 'em and squash 'em. You squash the cans by treading on them. This gives you more space for storage. Keep the cans in large cardboard boxes or paper sacks.

Who will pay for my cans?
Re-cycling centres will. Find out the address of your nearest Can Recycling Centre in the telephone book, or write to:

>Alican Recycling Scheme,
>Atcost Road,
>River Road,
>Barking,
>Essex IG11 0EQ

At the time of writing, re-cycling centres pay 40p per kilo or 40p for 50 cans. When you've collected a few hundred cans, take them along to the re-cycling centre to make your fortune.

The Metal Snake *

Make a fun metal snake with weird shapes. Use it as a percussion instrument, too.

You will need
a nail
a hammer
a thin length of string (long enough to run through all the cans)
a dozen aluminium cans

How to go about it

Ask an adult to knock a hole in the bottom of each can. Take great care because the edges of the cans are sharp. Thread the string through the cans. Tie a knot at each end. When you shake this instrument you create a rattlesnake!

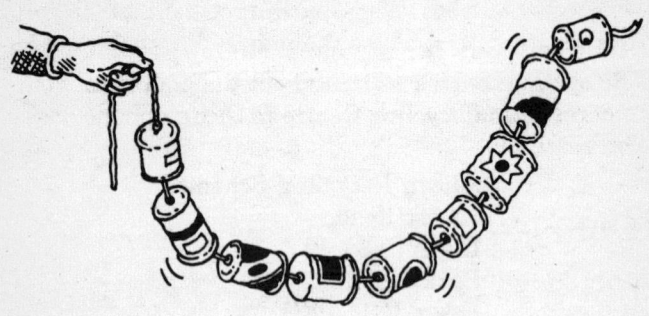

TEXTILES AND FABRICS

Any old or spoiled clothes you don't need? What do you do with them? Throw them out or take them to the jumble? There is an alternative. Why not use them for your own purposes?

Stuffing

No. Not the kind you sew up in the turkey, but the stuffing that goes into cushions. Old rags make excellent padding. Tear up some old clothes and stuff them in your cushions and pillows. If you have nice patterned rags you can sew them together to make cushion covers.

Notice-boards

Save any felt scraps for notice-boards. Find a piece of wood or chipboard as a backing. Glue the back of the felt pieces and attach them to the board. You can design a very attractive patchwork frame round the edge of the board and put your messages, notices and postcards in the centre.

Collage

Old bits of corduroy, carpeting and felt are ideal for collage. Glue the materials to the paper and arrange them attractively to achieve an amazing variety of surface textures.

PLASTICS

What do you do with plastic bottles when you've finished with them? Well, you could start up a small band. You have all the ingredients for a percussion instrument. Half fill your cleaned-out plastic bottles with small pebbles, dried beans, lentils, or a mixture of all three. Replace the top, then shake away and enjoy the music. (See 'Glass' waste, p. 15, for further additions to the 'Orchestra'.)

Egg-Boxes

You can use plastic egg-boxes to keep out the cold and loud sounds from your room. They are also good at keeping sound and heat in the room. Polystyrene egg-boxes work best as sound insulators. If you have a small room, pin up sheets of sugar paper to cover one of your walls. Glue the sticking-out parts of the

egg-boxes to the sugar paper and line them up in neat rows so you cover all the paper.

Wait until you have a good supply of egg boxes before you start your insulation project. You'll have more privacy and your music will sound better. Ask your friends for their egg-boxes. It'll save you eating too many eggs.

Plastic Containers

Small yogurt pots and margarine cartons make excellent containers for pens, pencils and paints.

A Yogurt Walkie-Talkie

Clean two yogurt cartons and make a hole in the centre of the base of each carton. Cut a long length of thick string. If you like, cut it long enough to stretch from one end of the house to the other.

Push one end of the string through the hole in one of the small cartons. Tie a knot so this end is well-secured. Do the same with the other carton. Hold the string taut and you have your walkie-talkie. The device will work well provided that you keep the string taut.

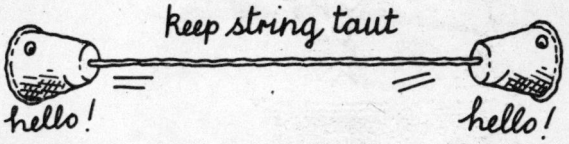

Feed Your Pets

Feed your pets from an empty plastic gallon can or any other plastic container. Ask an adult to cut a small bowl from the shape of the can. They will need a sharp knife or a pair of scissors. If you don't have a pet then you can use the shape as a paint bowl or a sailing-boat for the bath.

← cut here

useful for pet's feeding bowl

PAPER AND BOARD

Do you want to save trees, reduce pollution and conserve wildlife? Then start your own paper-save project. Many charities will support you and thank you for your efforts.

How to go about it

1 Get together a group of friends to help you.

2 Find a charity that would benefit from your paperchase.

3 Ask friends, family, neighbours and teachers to help by saving their newspapers and magazines.

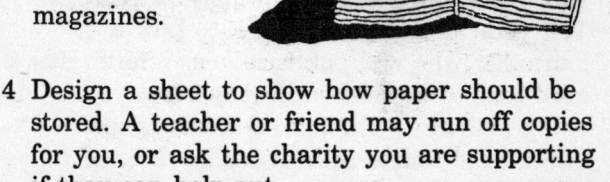

4 Design a sheet to show how paper should be stored. A teacher or friend may run off copies for you, or ask the charity you are supporting if they can help out.

a Stack the newspapers in close bundles so we can carry them easily.

b Bind the papers and magazines separately.

c Store in a cool dry place like a garage or garden shed. Keep well away from any naked flame.

5 Advertise your scheme as widely as possible. Tell your local paper and ask to talk to a journalist who will publicize your efforts. (It's a good idea to write down briefly what you're doing and why.) The local free newspaper is also a good source of information. Lots of people see advertisements in shop windows.

we're doing fantastic things for charities and conservation...

6 Make sure you have a large space where you can store the bundles of paper. If not, take them to the charity's shop or centre.

7 Arrange to collect the papers regularly. Collect at the same time on, say, the first Sunday in each month. If people are going to be out ask them to leave their bundles in a place where you can collect them easily.

When You've Read 'Em, Use 'Em

Painting your room? Keep a small bundle of newspapers to protect the floor and surfaces.
Packing? Crushed newspaper is very useful for packing glassware and other fragile objects.

Artistic? Have you ever tried collage? With collage you use different surfaces, pictures and materials. They are stuck in all sorts of arrangements to produce strange, wonderful and exciting designs. Newspapers and magazines contain pictures and print that you can use for unusual collages.

Cardboard Boxes

Well, what are cardboard boxes used for? Storing things, of course. Use them for toys, books, tools and papers. Paint them so they are an attractive addition to your room.

And when you've finished the corn-flakes, why not turn the stiff thin card of the box into masks. Make a face shape with eyes, nose and mouth. Paint the card and make two holes for string to tie the mask round your head.

Out Shopping

Many shop-keepers wrap their goods in small plastic or paper bags. This is a waste of paper. Take your own shopping bags and politely refuse paper bags when they are not necessary.

Re-Cycle Your Own Paper **

You will need
plenty of space
eight pages of good quality newspaper
a saucepan
washing-up liquid
a plastic washing-up bowl
a plastic bucket
a cooking ring
a dozen clean absorbent cloths
a liquidizer, (tell your parents what you're doing before you use the liquidizer. Make sure you wash it out thoroughly when you finish)
a square of thin wire mesh (about 20cm×20cm)
a colander
a big book
a wooden spoon
rubber gloves

How to go about it

1 Tear the newspaper into thin strips. Stuff them into the plastic bucket. Cover with water and leave to soak overnight.

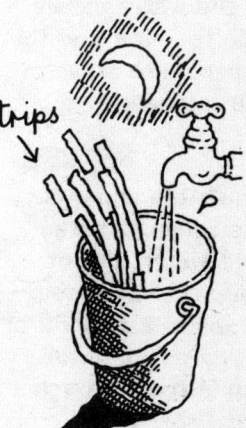

2 Pour out excess water. Transfer the paper into a medium sized saucepan, then cover the paper with fresh water. Add a spoonful of washing-up liquid.

3 Heat the mixture gently for two hours. (NB. Make sure the paper is always covered by the water.) Strain through a colander so the water passes into the sink and the paper mush stays in the colander.

4 Flush the paper in the colander with cold water. Put on your rubber gloves. Transfer a handful of soggy paper to the liquidizer. Add water until the liquidizer is three-quarters full.

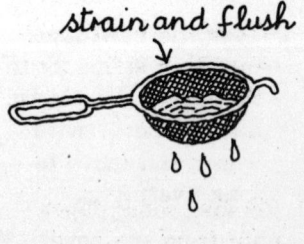

Switch on the liquidizer for a couple of seconds at a time until you have mixed in the paper for a total of one minute.

5 Liquidize all the paper as in instruction 4.

6 Transfer *all* the contents of the liquidizer to the plastic bowl. *Clean the liquidizer thoroughly.* Pour water into the bowl until it is half full and use the wooden spoon to stir the pulp into the water.

7 Remove some paper pulp from the bowl as in the picture.

Lay the absorbent cloth flat on a clean surface. Hold the mesh at an angle to the cloth. Quickly lay the mesh on the cloth with the pulp side down.

8 Press the mesh hard on to the cloth.

Peel off the mesh leaving the pulp behind.

9 Place another absorbent cloth on the pulp. Press hard. Repeat steps 7 and 8 on top of this cloth. Repeat until you have used up either the pulp or the cloths. Now you have a multi-layered cloth-pulp sandwich.

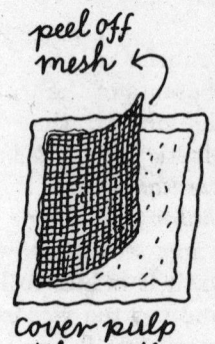

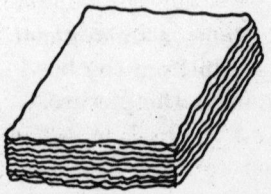

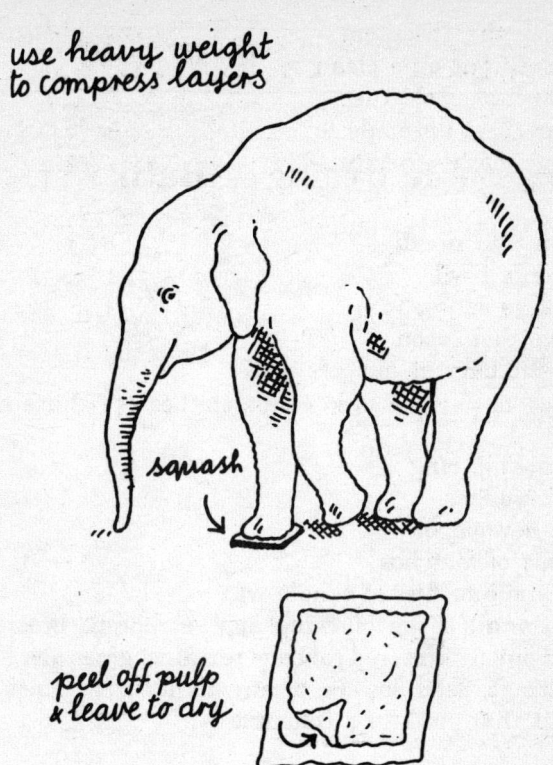

10 Lay a small plastic bag on top of the pile, then compress the 'sandwich' with a heavy book for a day. The pulp turns into paper. Peel off the damp sheets of paper from each cloth. Lay them on newspaper and leave them to dry.

Now you have lots of sheets of re-cycled paper which you can use to make things like birthday cards, posters, pictures for painting or letter-writing paper.

VEGETABLE WASTE

Vegetable dyeing – Batik **

You will need
a large bowl
a large saucepan
a wooden spoon
plastic bags or buckets
white or pale-coloured cotton clothes – T-shirts are ideal
a cooking ring
a colander
old newspaper
a box of matches
a candle or bits of candle wax
one, or all, of the following: apple scrapings, beetroot and onion skins, red cabbage remains, grass and leaf cuttings, dead flowers, or any plants, vegetables or fruit that produce a coloured dye

How to go about it
Keep the waste in separate plastic bags or buckets. There's no hard and fast rule about the waste material you use for dyeing. Experiment. You may get surprising results. It's difficult to predict the colour of the dye and this means it can be more fun. The colour depends on all sorts of things like the type of waste, its age, the time you leave the dye in water and the time you take to dye your clothes.

One interesting way of dyeing your clothes is called Batik. Here, waste candlewax makes all sorts of patterns.

Cover a clear area with old newspapers and spread your fabric on them. Produce designs by dripping molten candle wax on the fabric. For example, you could draw a funny face.

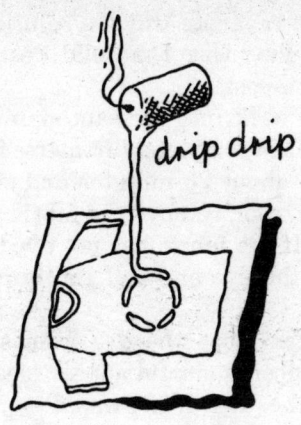

Wait for the wax to harden. Fold back your fabric so the wax cracks, then throw away the bits that flake off.

Half fill the saucepan with the waste plant, vegetable or fruit. Add a little water so you just cover it. Heat the contents of the pan gently and stir at intervals for at least 20 minutes. Place a large bowl under the colander. Pour the waste mixture in the pan through the colander to separate the dye solution from the vegetable residue. Use the solid residue in the colander for compost.

Pour the dye back into the saucepan and drop in your fabric so it is completely immersed in the dye. Boil gently for about 20 minutes and stir now and again. Allow to cool, remove the fabric and rinse it in cold water. If the fabric has not dyed completely put it back in the dye and boil gently for a further 15 minutes.

The candlewax stops the dye from staining the fabric so your design should appear clearly. Scrape off the rest of the wax. If the wax does not come off easily then it will melt if you touch it with the tip of a hot iron.

Drunken Cars

It's not the drivers in Brazil who should take a breathalyzer – it's the cars! Brazilian petrol is alcoholic. Yeast fungus breaks down sugar cane

which grows well in that area of South America. This process is called fermentation and is used to make wine as well as petrol!

Brazilian cars run on a mixture of unleaded petrol and 20 per cent alcohol. This cuts down on pollution and uses natural resources. If the cars break down they are probably drunk!

Muck-Raking: Compost For Healthier Plants **

What is compost?
It's a mixture of plant and animal remains. Sounds horrible? Well, the plants don't think so because it keeps their soil in good condition. Tiny germs attack the waste in the compost to release valuable foodstuffs. When you make a compost heap you start off a series of complicated and fascinating chemical reactions. Start your heap in April or May.

Why do plants like compost?
- It improves the soil.
- It supports the roots of plants.
- It makes the soil act like a sponge and improves drainage.
- It stops weeds growing.
- It keeps the soil moist.

What you need for a compost heap
A patch in your garden by a fence or wall. You will need a little shade but it should not be too damp.

An old piece of carpet or a black plastic bag to cover the heap and keep it moist.

An activator. This is a mixture that helps composting to start. You can buy them from garden shops or garden centres. Examples are 'Garotta' and QR or 'Quick Return' which is available from the Soil Association.

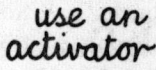
use an activator

Some lime to remove the acidity. This is available from gardening shops.

Six old bricks or planks to support the heap and allow air to circulate.

Woody twigs to re-inforce the base of the heap.

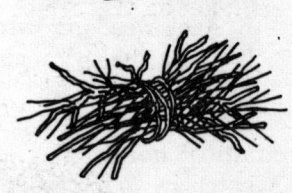

Soft waste. Material like cauliflower stems, orange peel, egg-shells, potato peelings, cabbage leaves, onion skins, old tea leaves, lawn cuttings, and if that's not enough, any other animal remains.

Other good ingredients for a compost heap are stinging nettles — wear rubber gloves to protect your hands — a little animal manure, crumpled paper (not glossy), weeds.

A bucket to collect your waste as you produce it.

Fibrous roots. When you dig over your garden remove roots and place them in a separate bucket to use on your heap.

Don't use!
Too many dead leaves. They take a long time to break down. Half a bucketful of leaves would be enough.
Cooked animal flesh.
Evergreen leaves.

How to go about it
Leave your waste in a bucket used only for compost. When it's full, you can empty the contents on the heap.

empty soft waste onto woody twigs

mix activator into waste

place bricks or planks 15cm apart

Find the right space in your garden. Compost heaps don't look very pretty so keep it in a corner of the garden.

Place six bricks about 15cm, apart. Arrange the twigs to form a layer on top of the bricks. This is the base of your heap.

Put a layer of soft waste on top of the twigs to a depth of 10cm. If you don't have enough waste, add as much as you can, cover it over with the carpet, then throw on more when you've collected it. Mix a little soil into the soft waste layer and sprinkle on a little activator and lime.

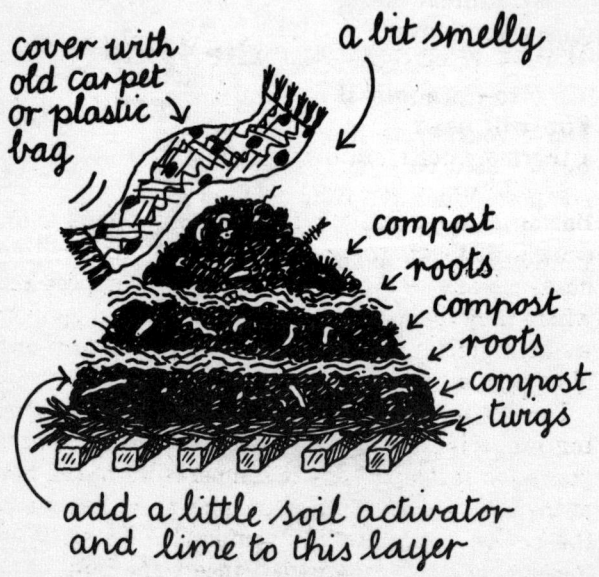

Now make a similar layer with fibrous roots, stinging nettles or crumpled paper – or a mixture of all three. Again, sprinkle on a little activator and lime. If you have a supply of horse manure add a spadeful now.

Continue to build up your heap in 'soft' and 'fibrous' layers for about three weeks. Protect the top of the heap with the carpet. When you've built up the heap leave it for about two months so the great chemical factory can get underway, then spread it over your garden. Take forkfuls of the compost and dig it in the soil near your plants.

Your flourishing garden will make your efforts worthwhile.

What happens in the heap? *

You will need
a thermometer from 0°C – 100°C

Bacteria, fungi and other microscopic living things can't wait to get their chemical juices on dead and decaying material. They work on the compost heap where they release all the nutrients locked up in the waste material. Insects, small mammals and birds also have an interest in compost heaps.

The thermometer will tell you if the heap is working properly and has a life of its own. As soon as you've built it up take the temperature of the heap at the same time and the same place each day during the period you allow the compost to fester. When measuring the temperature, insert the bulb of the thermometer into the heap until the temperature remains steady, then record your result like this:

Day	Temperature°C
1	14
2	16
3	15

If your heap is working properly you will find that the temperature rises for a number of days, then it starts to go down. Note any changes you see in the heap when you measure the temperature. Your compost heap will become quite hot on some days.

The Compost Zoo

What kind of animals like compost? You will be amazed at the animals attracted to your living rubbish heap. Make a list of the different animals you find. Don't disturb the heap too much. You'll find a lot of fascinating insect life in the surface layers. If you find an animal you can't recognize, make a note of the number of legs, shape of body and any unusual features. Identify it using a book from the library. You will make some unusual discoveries.

Explosive Compost

It's not just gardeners that have always used compost. During the English Civil War explosives manufacturers were desperate for compost. In 1646 they extracted chemicals called nitrates from the compost to produce . . . gunpowder!

Make Your Own Power Station ***

Rotting vegetables and manure are great sources of energy. They produce a gas called methane which is the gas that comes out of the holes in your cooker. It is a fuel, and when you apply a flame it burns to give out heat and light. Methane and the other gases from rotting waste are known as *biogas* which means 'living gas'. Collect this gas, and you have your free supply of fuel!

> *Important*: Do this project at school with the help of a teacher. Follow the instructions very carefully. Make sure an adult helps you with each step.

You will need
a pair of rubber gloves
two small black plastic bags
a length of T-shaped glass tubing with a glass jet attached. The tubing must have a 3-way tap. (Your science teacher at school should have this item.)
two rubber bands
a brick or a large book
a supply of horse manure. Try the local stables or a generous gardener. (You'll need a cupful)
a supply of rotting veg. The contents of your compost bucket would be ideal
a little pond sludge

How to go about it

1 Put a cupful of manure into one of the plastic bags. Add a handful of rotting vegetables and enough pond sludge to moisten the solid mixture. Wash your hands carefully after you have carried out this step.

2 Squeeze the empty part of the bag to expel any air. Tie the bag to one end of the T-shaped tubing with the rubber band.

3 Flatten out the empty plastic bag to exclude as much air as possible. Attach this bag to the other end of the glass tubing.

Leave the equipment set up for three weeks in a fairly warm place. Bacteria work on the decaying vegetables and the horse manure and start to release biogas. You should see the empty bag expanding as it fills up with the gas from the sludgy mixture.

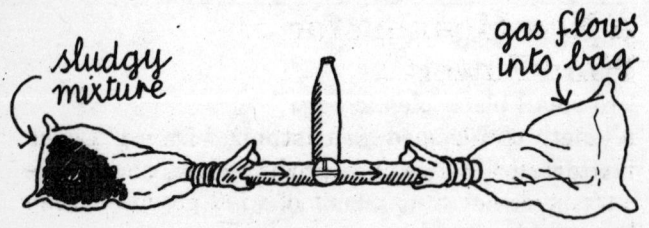

When the bag has swollen — but not to the point of bursting — you are ready to burn the biogas. Turn the three-way tap so the gas can run to the jet. Place a heavy object on the expanded bag to squeeze it and force the biogas through the glass jet. You *must* allow gas to run through for a few seconds, then an adult should apply a flame just above the end of the jet. The gas will burn. There may be an energy crisis in the world, but you have created your own supply of free energy.

Heat a small pan of water above the flame and boil yourself an egg. Make yourself a cup of coffee and have a bio-breakfast!

A New Meaning for Wind Power

A New Zealand scientist, Dr David Lowe, investigated the wind produced by sheep. He estimated that the amount of wind produced daily by a single sheep contains enough methane gas to run a small truck for twenty-five miles. He claimed New Zealand could solve its fuel problems if it could find a way to harness this output. Have you any brilliant ideas? If so, New Zealand awaits your call. However, I doubt if the sheep would be very happy with you!

A Nibble For The Rabbit

If you have a rabbit or any other vegetarian pet then here's a recipe. Feed them a nice rich concoction of silage. During summer when you mow the lawn, allow the cuttings to dry in the sun before you place them in an airtight container like a bin-liner. Flatten the bag after you have put in the cuttings to push out air, then tie it. When you have more lawn cuttings open the bag, pour them in, flatten and tie again. Leave the contents for three weeks, then dole out as animal feed.

Dust and Cinders

These can be used on a slippery patch in icy weather.

Acids Are Innocent, OK?

Nowadays we hear a lot about acid rain in the news. But what is it and where does it come from? Well, it is formed when acid gases, the waste of coal-fired power stations, escape and mingle with rain. This mixture then causes a lot of damage to our environment. To give you an idea of how dangerous acid rain can be, just remember that most undiluted acids are corrosive, which means that they produce a burning sensation if you touch them (don't!) and can even dissolve some metals like iron and zinc.

Acids are, however, also very important. Strong acids like sulphuric acid and nitric acid are used to make fertilizers, dyes and detergents. Vinegar is a weak acid that we use for pickling and flavouring

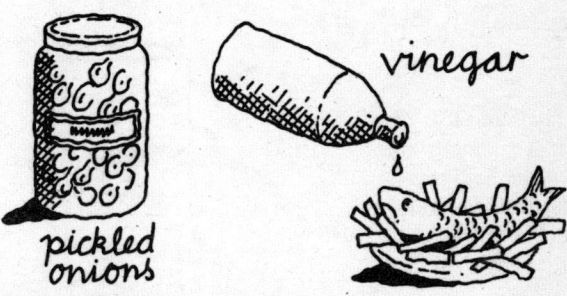

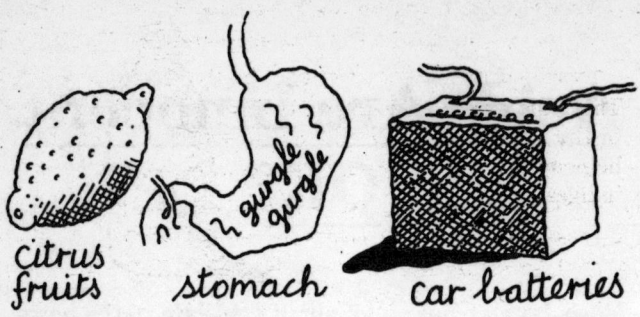

food. There are also harmless acids in our body that help our blood and body cells to function properly. In our stomach, there's even a strong acid similar to hydrochloric acid. This helps to break down fragments of food so they can be digested more easily. Car batteries, too, run on acids. They react chemically with a metal to produce an electric current. So acids do not always mean bad news.

In this chapter you can find out all about acids and acid rain, through lots of exciting experiments. So read on . . .

There are other chemicals that have a dramatic effect when they mix with acids. They are the acid killers, otherwise known as *alkalis*. Here are some examples:

This contains crystals of a strong alkali called sodium hydroxide. Among other things it is used to clear drains.

This kills excess acid in the stomach. It helps to cure indigestion.

milk of magnesia

Gardeners and farmers use lime to make soils less acid.

lime

The Taste Test *

What is the simplest way to recognize an acid? Taste it. Stop! Don't drink the acid in a car battery – you won't live to tell the tale. Many acids are safe to taste but you must only try those that are listed in the instructions below.

Collect the following substances, or as many as you can, which you should find in your home. Clear a space in the kitchen and place them together on a paper towel.

You will need

a lemon
tomato paste
an orange
a sliver of soap
a ripe apple
an unripe apple
buttermilk
bicarbonate of soda
  or baking powder
a bottle of sauce
natural yogurt (no sugar)
a grapefruit
tap water
juice from pickled
  cucumbers
toothpaste
vinegar
soda water

You will also need
a few plastic teaspoons
plastic or paper cups

What happens
You may have noticed that acids we eat and drink have one thing in common. They taste sour. This will be our test for an acid — sourness. Those substances that taste sour we'll call acids. Remember that sugar and other ingredients can mask sourness, so take this into account. Test each substance for a few seconds on your tongue before deciding whether it is an acid or not. Record your results, with these headings, in a table like this:

Sour Tasting	Not Sour Tasting
Lemon	Soap

Carry out this experiment with your friends. People have different 'tastes' so make sure you agree on the description of sourness.

Acid Teeth *

Have you, a friend, brother or sister recently lost a tooth? Why don't you use it to do a disappearing act with the help of a bottle of cola?

Teeth are very hardy. They are built to survive most of the stuff you put into your mouth. But some sweets and drinks do give teeth a hard time. Here is a dramatic example of the way sweet acid drinks can damage your teeth.

Drop your tooth in a plastic cup and pour in cola until it just covers it. Examine the tooth at the end of each day. After a week you will see why brushing teeth is an important part of health care.

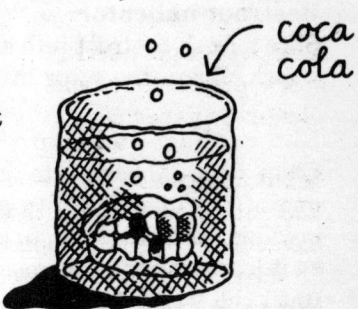

What happens
The acid helps to dissolve the tooth. Certain germs thrive in the acid conditions the cola provides. These germs feed on the outer covering of your tooth, which is called enamel, and gradually destroy it. That's what happens to fizzy drink lovers who don't brush their teeth.

The Colour Test *

Is tasting a reliable way of recognizing acids? Remember, sugar can turn sour into sweet. Your friends may disagree about sourness, too. The tongue is not a very good indicator.

Find out if your results were accurate by using a chemical indicator. These are dyes or pigments that change when you add them to acids or alkalis.

The best known laboratory indicator is litmus. It comes in the form of paper or as a solution. Your teacher may have litmus paper in school and may let you have some. Or how about making your own chemical indicator? Two of the best home-made indicators are red cabbage and beetroot.

Beetroot indicator
Slice a fresh beetroot into a clean bowl. Mash it with a fork. Drain the juice into a clean cup.

Red cabbage indicator
Chop a red cabbage into quarters. Carefully cut up one of the quarters into as many small pieces as possible. Transfer them to a saucepan and add water so it just covers the pieces. Gently heat the mixture until the water turns a deep violet colour.

The chart below is a guide to the colours of indicators in acids, alkalis and substances that are neither acid nor alkali – i.e. neutral.

Colours

Indicator	Acid	Neutral	Alkali
red litmus	stays red	stays red	turns blue
blue litmus	turns red	stays blue	stays blue
red cabbage	red	violet	green
beetroot	_____	_____	_____

Fill in the colours for beetroot. Gather together the substances you used for the Taste Test (see page 47). This time test each substance with a chemical indicator. If you use litmus paper place a little of each specimen in a cup and dip in the paper. If the specimen is a solid or powder add a little water and shake so it can dissolve.

When you use a liquid indicator like beetroot, red cabbage or litmus solution pour a little indicator on to each substance and note down the colour change. Wash out the cup thoroughly after each test. Record your results on a table like the one below.

Name of Indicator:

Specimen	Indicator Colour	Ac/Alk/Neu	Taste Test
Vinegar	Litmus turns red	Acid	sour/Acid

Acid Killers in Action *

How can we get rid of the acid in acid rain? Answer: employ an acid killer. You won't need to look through the Yellow Pages to find one. An alkali will do the job.

What happens when an alkali meets an acid? You can see the whole murky spectacle in the comfort of your own kitchen. Pour any acid solution – for example vinegar – into a plastic cup until it is about a quarter full. Add a few drops of indicator solution to prove it's an acid. With a teaspoon, add a little bicarbonate of soda to the acid. Continue adding and mixing the bicarbonate of soda until there is no further change.

Bicarbonate of soda is an alkali, of course. It neutralizes the acid. This means it converts the acid into the neutral substance, water. The fizzing you see is due to the gas carbon dioxide. When you have finished with your mixture throw it down the sink and clean out the cup thoroughly.

This experiment mimics the chemistry in your stomach when you take indigestion tablets or powders. Bicarbonate of soda is just such a powder. When you suffer from indigestion your stomach becomes too acid. Indigestion tablets are alkalis you send to your stomach to neutralize the acid. Bicarbonate of soda is used in baking also. When heated it breaks up and releases carbon dioxide gas. The gas expands and makes your bread and cakes rise.

In Sweden the lakes are sprayed with lime. Since lime neutralizes acids, this helps to restore the natural balance in lakes that have been poisoned by acid rain.

Burning Rain

Even in the cleanest air the rain is acid. Part of our atmosphere consists of carbon dioxide gas – it's the stuff we breathe out. The gas dissolves in those great banks of water vapour called clouds. Carbon dioxide makes the water slightly acid so rain is naturally acid.

Scientists can measure acidity. They have a scale

to tell them how acid a substance is just as a scale of temperature tells us how hot something is. The scale for acidity is called pH. It has numbers from 0 to 14.

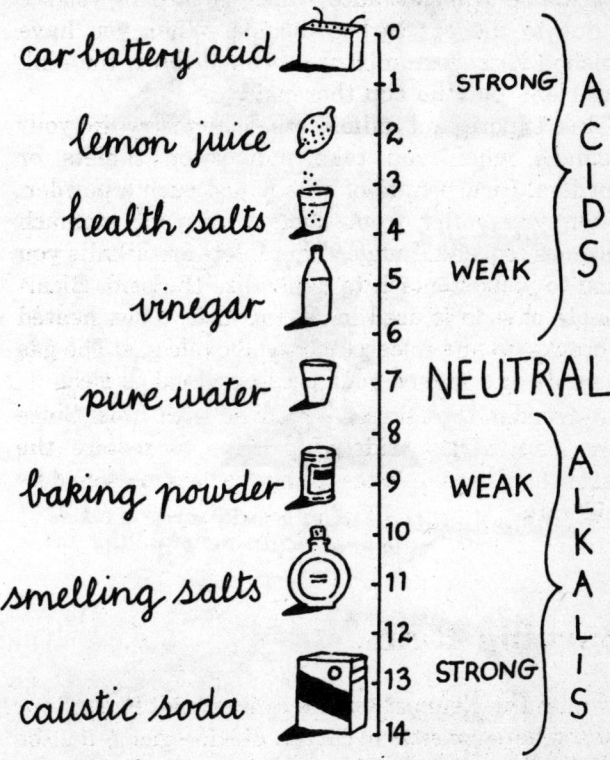

An acid can have any pH number under 7. Stronger acids have lower pH numbers than weak acids.

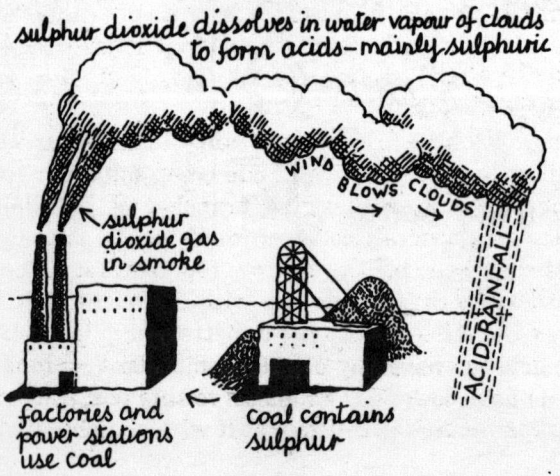

Until the Industrial Revolution in the late eighteenth century the pH of rain had probably never fallen below pH 5. Then, in the late nineteenth century, a chemist called Angus Smith discovered that the rainfall in Manchester contained quantities of a very corrosive acid called sulphuric acid. And the reason for this was the unrestricted burning of coal for home fires and industry.

Collect Your Own Acid Rain **

How acid is the rain falling on you? You will need a special kind of indicator to find out. There are two types of indicator you could use. Ask your teacher if he or she can supply you with narrow range universal indicator paper. This indicator not only tells you whether you have an acid or not – it also signifies how acid a substance is, or its pH value. You can also obtain a special acid drop measuring-kit from WATCH (*see page 120*). This will give you accurate results.

Now you have to collect the rain. This is not as easy as it sounds because water can creep into your rain collector from overhanging branches or buildings. Make your own rain collector from a plastic lemonade bottle and cut off the narrow top cleanly. Ask an adult to do this job for you with a sharp knife.

Fix the collector at least a metre (three feet) from the ground, well away from any object that could drip water into it. A post would serve this purpose, and you can secure the collector to it with a rubber band.

Insert a small clean plastic bag open inside the bottle to make sure your collecting vessel is perfectly clean.

When you have set up your equipment, measure the pH in the evening of each rainy day. Don't get soaked! Put in a new plastic bag each time and continue the experiment for seven different days at least. Record your results in a table like the one below, and tick the correct column. Keep your samples of rain. You will need them for the experiments on page 59.

DATE	pH 5–6	pH 4.6–4.9	pH 4.3–4.6	under pH 4.3
2nd Nov. 1986	✓			

It is known that wind direction can influence the acidity of the rain. When easterly winds blow from Europe the rain is much more acid than rain blown in from the Atlantic. The easterly winds carry the acid gases from European countries. The Atlantic westerlies blow in cleaner rain.

If your rain is below pH 4.3 it's very acid and it's time to find out why. Make a record of any unusual weather conditions if your rain is acid.

Home-Made Acid Rain *

As well as collecting acid rain you can make your own. All you need is a small Campden tablet. You can buy these in any chemist's shop that sells wine-making equipment. They are used to sterilize glass vessels.

Pour a little tap-water into a small plastic container. Crush the tablet, pop it into the container and replace the lid. Slosh the water gently to dissolve the tablet. Leave the container for half an hour. Quickly remove and replace the lid to check the tablet has dissolved. The tablet releases sulphur dioxide gas in water so it is what you would expect to collect after an acid rainfall. Save this acid water for later experiments.

If you spill any of this acid wash it away with plenty of tap-water. Your 'acid rain' is poisonous and *dangerous to taste or drink*.

The Acid Match

Every time a match is struck more acid enters the atmosphere. The match head contains sulphur. When sulphur burns it produces sulphur dioxide – the main cause of acid rain.

Speaking As A Plant **

'It's all right for us humans to go on about acid rain. We don't have to stand with muddy acid rain-water up to our waists day in and day out. Sounds absurd? Not to the poor old plants it doesn't. After all, their roots have to struggle with the soil into which the acid rain falls. If they could talk, maybe they could tell us a thing or two about acid rain.

Many politicians and industrialists deny that acid rain does damage to our plant and animal life. They

say: 'Well, you see, the fact of the matter is that, er, you know, there is no definite evidence that proves acid rain does damage to our trees . . . many factors could be responsible. . . .'

It is true that there are many things in the air that could harm plants. However, there is definite proof that acid rain, and nothing else, damages living things.

We can speak for the plants by finding out how acid rain alone affects them. This means carrying out a control experiment. Scientists are always performing this type of experiment. It's much easier than it sounds. It means growing two sets of plants under exactly the same conditions. You give them the same amount of light and heat. There is only one difference. One set of plants you water regularly, the other you water at exactly the same time but with ingredients like acid rain-water.

You will need:
eight small plastic cups or glass jars (they should all be the same size)
a supply of barley or cress seedlings (20–40)
absorbent paper, e.g. kitchen paper
acid rain-water from the project on pages 56–7
rain-water with the lowest pH from the project on page 55
a little gardening lime or crushed chalk
crushed egg-shell
bicarbonate of soda
a small ruler

What happens
Moisten a sheet of the absorbent paper with tap-water. The paper must be neither too damp nor too dry. Sprinkle the paper with water. Don't soak it. Crumple the paper gently and poke it to the bottom of the cup or jar. Place three or four seedlings on the paper as far apart from each other as possible. When the paper starts to dry out moisten it by sprinkling on fresh water.

Plant a set of seedlings in the same way in the other containers, but with the following changes to the basic instructions:

2nd container: Moistened paper with acid rain-water from project on pages 56–7.

3rd container: Moistened paper with acid rain-water from project on page 55.

4th container: To two dessertspoons of the acid rain-water you made (page 56) add half a dessertspoon of lime and stir in. Use this mixture to moisten the paper.

5th container: As for the 2nd container but sprinkle crushed egg-shell around the paper. Don't get the egg-shell over the seedlings.

6th container: As for the 2nd container, then sprinkle on a little lime after the first leaves have sprouted.

7th container: Moisten the paper with a dilute solution of bicarbonate of soda.

8th container: A concoction of your own choice.

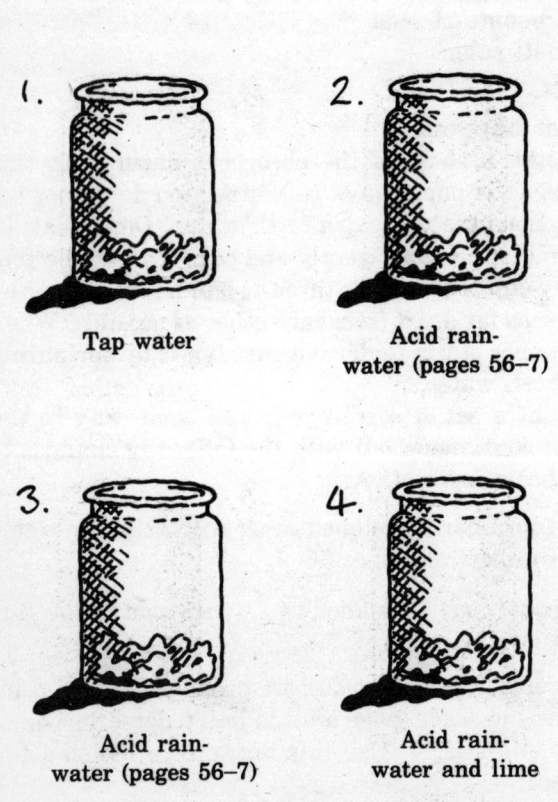

1. Tap water
2. Acid rain-water (pages 56–7)
3. Acid rain-water (pages 56–7)
4. Acid rain-water and lime

Position the containers by a window where they are exposed to equal light and warmth. Remember to moisten the absorbent paper with the same solution each time it starts to dry. For example, you should only replenish the 7th container with bicarbonate of soda solution.

Wait for the seedlings to germinate. This happens when the shoot sprouts through the seed coat and the tiny leaves start to grow. Then make a report on a table like the one on the next page.

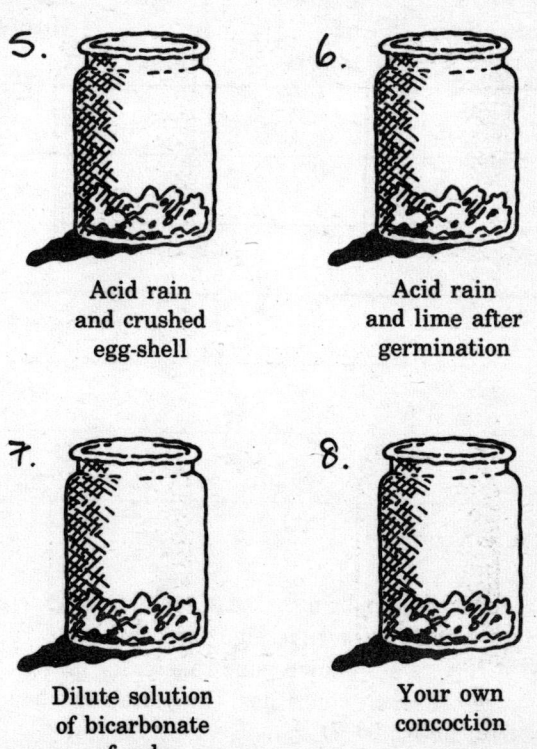

5. Acid rain and crushed egg-shell

6. Acid rain and lime after germination

7. Dilute solution of bicarbonate of soda

8. Your own concoction

Make a record on the growth of the seedlings for each solution.

Solution: Tap-water

Reason: Control. Ideal conditions

Time after germination (days)	Colour of leaves	Height of shoot	Any Mould?
0			
3			
6			
9			
12			
15			

These records will be a source of important information for your further investigations into acid rain. Make sure you note down your reason for using the substances in each container. (Egg-shell is used to neutralize acids.)

Solution: 'Acid Rain'

Reason: To see the effect of 'acid rain' on germinating seedlings

The Soil-Builders **

It's not just plants that have to put up with acid rain. Earthworms, snails, centipedes and other tiny creepy-crawlies spend a lifetime burrowing in the soil. These little animals are very important. They turn over the soil so it is thoroughly aired. They renew the topsoil and help to re-cycle nutrients. Without them our plant life would wither and die. They are a meal for many of our birds too.

You will need
a large plastic tray, at least 50cm×50cm
a pair of wellies
a pair of rubber gloves
a trowel
soapy water
a large plastic carton
a supply of 'acid rain-water' and lime. (For acid rain-water see pages 56–7.)

What happens
Collect earth worms and other easily identifiable animals like woodlice. Make a pitfall trap – see pages 101–2. To bring earthworms to the surface pour a little soapy water over the soil in your garden or other

patch. Place any other tiny animals you find in the plastic container you use for your pitfall trap.

When you have collected at least thirty animals cover the base of the tray with soil up to a depth of 3cm, (1in) or more. Put the tray in a shed or other sheltered place.

Divide your tray into four quarters:

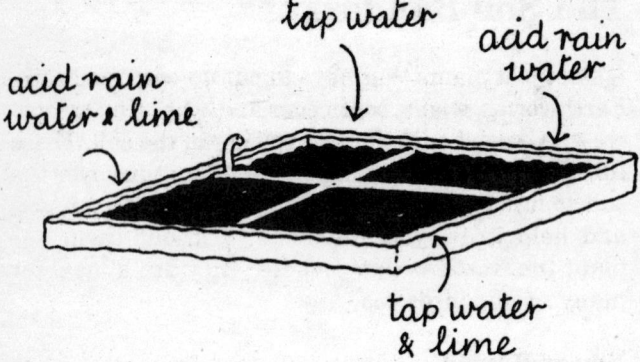

1st quarter: Keep moist with tap-water.

2nd quarter: Keep moist with 'acid rain-water'.

3rd quarter: Sprinkle powdered chalk or lime over the surface of the soil. Moisten with tap-water.

4th quarter: Sprinkle powdered chalk or lime over the soil. Moisten with 'acid rain-water'.

With care put your creepy crawlies in the middle of the tray. It does not matter if there are small animals in there all ready. Note how they distribute themselves in a table like this.

Numbers of animals

Time (hours)	Part 1	Part 2	Part 3	Part 4
0	12	10	10	15
1				
2				
3				
4				
5				
6				

Count the number of animals in each part at hourly intervals. When you have finished put the animals back in the soil of your garden or wherever you found them.

Did the animals prefer any particular soil? What did the animals have to tell you about the effects of acid rain?

Which Soil? **

Do our hardworking soil animals prefer a particular soil? If you find out, then you could do a lot to help them. This experiment looks at the animals in different kinds of soils.

Collect soil from four different habitats. The following four provide a good range.

1 Garden soil
2 Soil from a deciduous wood. That's a wood with broad-leaved trees like oak, ash and beech.
3 Soil from a conifer wood. That is a wood with trees bearing needle-shaped leaves like the pine and larch.
4 Soil by a stagnant ditch.

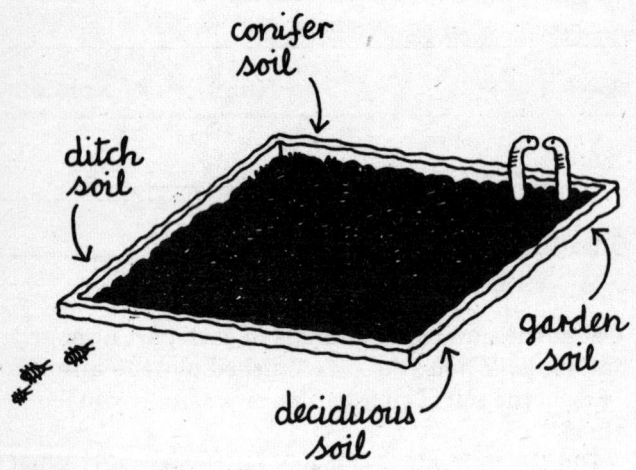

You will need
a bucket to carry the soil back to your 'laboratory'
a pair of wellies, especially if it's damp
a pair of rubber gloves
a trowel
a large plastic tray
somewhere like a shed to carry out your investigations

What happens

Collect the different soils using your trowel. Don't take more than you need. Arrange them in the tray as sketched in the diagram but don't pack the soil too closely. Animals like to move through the soil without having to drill a path for themselves.

Repeat the experiment in The Soil-Builders (page 63) but this time leave the animals for twenty-four hours before you make your own record of where they gather in a table like this.

Soil	Numbers of animals
garden	
deciduous	
conifer	
ditch	

Soil that the animals seem to avoid:

Soil that the animals seem to like:

When you have recorded your results find out whether the soils are acid or not.

You will need
strips of universal paper and narrow range paper, see
   Collect Your Own Acid Rain (page 55)
four empty jam-jars with lids
an old spoon

What happens
Transfer a spoonful of soil to a jar and cover the soil with tap water. Replace the lid and shake the jar vigorously. Leave each sample for a couple of days. Allow the soil to settle. Test a little water in each jar with the indicator paper and note the exact pH in a table like this.

Type of soil	pH value
garden	
deciduous	
conifer	
ditch	

Don't stop there. You have more investigating to do. You can change the pH of an acid soil by adding an alkali like lime. You can take the pH up to 7 or more by doing this. Try it with an acidic soil and note if it makes any difference to the movement of the animals.

Living Indicators In Dead Places **

Lichens are very useful. They are colourful, fungus-like plants that grow well on the barks of trees and gravestones. Lichens tell us whether the air is full of acid sulphur dioxide or whether it is very clean. Certain lichens will grow only where the air is thoroughly nasty, full of sulphur dioxide and grime. They thrive on acid rain. Scientists call them *acidophilous* which means they are fond of acids.

Other lichens have a more normal taste. They like their air reasonably clean but can tolerate a little acid. The final category are very fussy. They grow only in the cleanest air. Acid rain kills them.

Graveyards are the best places to go lichen-hunting. Here, trees and stones remain undisturbed so the lichens flourish. When you explore your local graveyard a search for lichens should help you answer the question: Is acid rain a problem in my area?

A guide to lichens

Crusty lichens grow on trees and acid stonework in patches. They stick well to the surface and like acids.

crusty lichen has powdery texture

Leafy lichens grown on alkaline stonework like limestone and tolerate acid rain.

Shrubby lichens grow only in the cleanest air. They stick loosely to the trees and stones on which they grow.

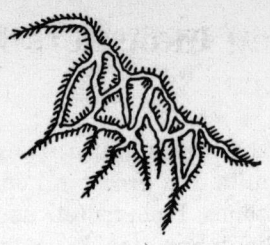

The diagram shows the three main types of lichens. The crusty lichens stick like a crust in irregular patches to the surfaces on which they grow. They are also very crumbly. Crusty lichens indicate dirty air.

The leafy lichens are like large fancy-coloured leaves. Many grow in limestone. Leafy lichens can be a little deceptive because limestone can neutralize acids. This means they can grow in areas where the air is fairly acid. They indicate areas where the air is neither too acid nor too clean.

Shrubby lichens have a stringy appearance and are loosely attached to the surface. They only grow in the cleanest air. Shrubby lichens are good news.

Don't remove any lichens. They take a long time to grow and will be of interest to other lichen-spotters.

Try and cover as many graveyards in your area as possible. Walk, use your bike or take a bus. Watch out for any differences between graveyards. If crusty lichens seem to be taking over look out for any nearby sources of pollution.

Make a record of your findings on a table like the one on the next page.

Name of graveyard: Corpsefield churchyard

Date: 31/5/86

Name of area: Newtown

Type of area: near industrial site/ centre of city/ outskirts of city/ small town/ village/ lonely country spot

Small town

Any possible sources of pollution: Brewery on outskirts of town

Type of lichen	Number of different lichens
crusty	3
leafy	9
shrubby	2

A graveyard may vary in the types of lichens grown. Some parts may be full of crusty lichens and others mainly shrubby. Try and find out the reasons for this.

You may wish now to carry out a more detailed study of lichens. The British Museum of Natural History have published a guide to lichens – from those that grow in the most polluted air to those that prefer the least pollution. See page 128. You will need a hand lens to help you look closely at each lichen.

The Case Against Acid Rain **

It doesn't matter where you live – city or village – acid rain attacks metals, joints, bricks, stones, rivers and ornamental ponds. Old churches are full of character and could tell a story or two about acid rain:

'Twenty years ago I had a fine grey skin. Sparkling it was. And full of beautiful statues. Yes. I was the pride and joy of the town. Then one day it rained. Well, I like rain, but this rain was different. Normally rain gets rid of all the dirt that settles on my stones, but this rain stung. It hurt. I was glad when it stopped. Each time it rained it hurt more, so I was scared when the sky turned grey. I discovered that bits of me were dissolving. All my stonework was pock-marked. And the statues! They lost their eyes, ears and noses. I'm st a r ting to f a   ll   ap   ar t . . .'

Many churches and old buildings could tell the same story. Look for the evidence in your own area. If your church boasts gargoyles or statues on its walls, take a careful look to see if they have worn away. Look for corrosive patches on ironwork like gates and railings. They rust in acid rain even when protected by sand-blasting and paint.

Make a record of your survey. Use the table below as a guide.

Buildings affected by acid rain

Name of building: Grimfield Town Hall

Function: Runs the town

Approximate date of construction: 1902

Points of interest: Limestone facade

Materials on outside of building: limestone, mortar, iron bars by window

Damage seen: Limestone worn away. Iron rusty

Indicator lichens on walls and in churchyard: Mainly crusty. A few leafy

The Rain That Hit The Roof

Most of Poland's electricity is produced in a great industrial area called Katowice. The furnaces in the power-stations burn coal and produce acidic gases as waste. East winds blast these clouds of gas down to Cracow. Cracow is the home of a gold-roofed cathedral, the pride and joy of the city.

The great clouds of acid settle above Cracow because it is in a valley. When the clouds break they unload a cocktail of strong acid rain in the city. This has ruined many buildings, but the cathedral suffered spectacular damage – over the years the gold roof slowly disappeared in the rain.

This was alarming news because it's no ordinary acid that dissolves gold. There's only one acid that can do it. It's called *aqua regia* and it is a mixture of concentrated nitric acid and hydrochloric acid – two of the most dangerous acids. *Aqua regia* means 'royal water'. It is the only chemical that can dissolve that royal metal, gold.

Umbrellas are useless against this rain. What chance do they stand against such a dangerous chemical? Now the citizens of Cracow are hitting the roof before their entire city dissolves.

A Sour Case

Acid Rain stands guilty of the following charges:

1. Destroying important food crops. It kills the cells in the leaves of these plants so they cannot make food.

2 Killing forests. Acid Rain removed many important minerals from the soil. These minerals are important for the health of trees.

3 Poisoning trees. Acid Rain releases chemicals containing aluminium from the soil. Aluminium attacks and poisons the roots of trees.

4 Poisoning lakes and killing great stocks of fish. Fish cannot live in acid lakes.

5 Attacking buildings. It has cost a tremendous amount of money to repair and restore these buildings.

A Rosey Defence

But is Acid Rain all bad? Surprisingly, some gardeners may welcome acid rain. It protects roses. A nasty fungus called Black Spot attacks the leaves of roses. Black Spot likes clean, non-acid air so it cannot survive an acid shower. If your roses are nice and healthy then it may be due to the effect of Acid Rain.

Are Habitats Habitable?

Unless you live in the middle of the desert you should find a source of fresh water near where you live. This source could be a stream, river, canal, lake, gravel-pit or pond. Even in the middle of a large city fresh water can be an important habitat for many forms of wildlife. A *habitat* is the natural home of a plant or animal. Here they live surrounded by food and shelter. Destroy the habitat and you destroy the wildlife. It takes time for plants and animals to adjust to a new habitat.

In some areas, the local authorities impose strict rules about pollutants and waste, whilst others allow their wildlife to die off. And that's where you come in!

Is your local authority doing its job? Find out how they treat your local wildlife. Spend a sunny afternoon by your local river and you could come across skipping voles, water rats, swans, mallard ducks, reed bunting and herons. It should be well stocked with fish, too.

In some areas, streams and rivers have become nothing more than running sewers and chemical baths. This means they are harming your environment, destroying habitats and spoiling your fun. It's time to take ACTION!

First, you need to collect evidence about the freshwater life in your area. If you are investigating a river or canal, carry out your survey at three different points as in the following project:

Is Your River Clean or Polluted? *

You will need
a pair of rubber gloves
a pond net
a plastic pot or jar
a pH stick or universal indicator paper
a small trowel

How to go about it
Make an initial checklist of any signs of pollution. Copy the table below. Tick the box which describes the water most accurately.

Signs of clear water		Signs of polluted water	
1 Water looks clear	☐	Water looks dirty	☐
2 Little or no floating litter	☐	Lots of floating litter	☐
3 †No oil	☐	Oil slicks on surface	☐
4 Plenty of living things in water	☐	Few living things in water	☐
5 A wide variety of plant life at the verge	☐	Few different plants at verge	☐
6 pH neutral or alkaline	☐	pH acid	☐
7 Mud smells pleasant	☐	Mud smells horrible	☐

† On a sunny day you will see a rainbow effect on the surface of the water if oil is present.

Test 4 Run the net through the water and empty the contents into the plastic container. Repeat this two more times. Count as many different small animals as you can. If you count more than three different species this is an indication of clean water.

Test 5 Clean and dry the plastic container. Use it to scoop up a small sample of water. Dip in the pH stick or universal indicator paper and record the colour. If the pH is 7 or above then this is a sign of clean water.

Test 7 Using the trowel, remove a little mud from the bank of the river below the water line or from the bottom if it is very shallow. Hold it at arm's length from your nose and sniff.

If you have ticked all the seven signs for clean water then you're in luck. Your river is healthy and well. Any ticks for polluted water? On to the next project!

How Dirty Is The Water? **

You will need
a long piece of transparent plastic tubing, with a plastic lid for at least one end. The long narrow tubes for posters are ideal. Try a shop that sells posters, a bookshop or a large stationer
a pair of rubber gloves
a plastic bucket
an old cup or beaker
an oil-base felt-tip pen
a ruler

What happens

Clear water isn't always healthier than murky water. Very clear water means problems because it indicates that there are no plants or animals. Water that supports life should be a little murky.

Dirty water is a nuisance for living things. Muddy particles clog the gills of fish and impede their breathing. They also stop sunlight penetrating beyond the surface layers of the water.

Do this experiment with friends. See who can find the dirtiest water, but no cheating! Collect water from your local source of fresh water. Swish the water around the surface, being careful not to stir up the mud at the bottom. You will need about three-quarters of a bucketful of water. Your friends should take similar samples from other locations.

Remove any large pieces of litter. There should be two plastic lids at both ends of the plastic tubing. Remove one, draw a big cross on the inside of the lid then replace it. Take off the other lid. You won't need it.

Carry out this experiment in the open. A garden is a good place.

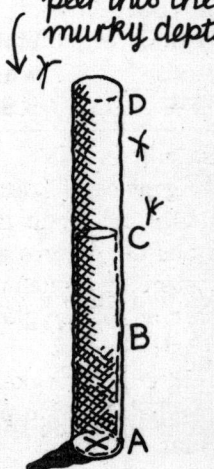

peer into the murky depths

Look through the open end of the tubing so you can see the cross at the bottom.

Hold the tube vertically. Draw water from the bucket with the cup, making sure you swish the bucket first. Pour a

little water down the
tubing. Look at the cross
through the water. Can
you still see it? Continue
to pour water down the
tubing until you cannot
see the cross. If you can
still see the cross when
the water has reached
the top of the tubing
then the water is clean.

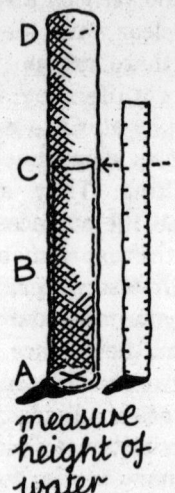

When the cross
disappears from view,
stop pouring water and
measure the height of
the water in the tubing.

measure height of water

Record your result in a table
like the one below.

Location of water	Height of water when x disappears	Cleanliness of water
Spring river	10cm	Rather dirty

When you have a result empty the tubing and
clean it out with tap water. Compare your
friends' samples.
  One way of recording the cleanliness of the
water is to divide the tubing into thirds.

Water which makes the cross disappear before it reaches B call *FILTHY*.

Between B and C the water is *DIRTY*.

Between C and D the water is *FAIRLY CLEAN*.

Above D, no problem! The water is *CLEAN*.

Can Life Breathe in Water?

The answer is 'Yes' – as long as oxygen is present. Some rivers are so filthy they contain hardly any oxygen gas. There are some tiny germs and small plants that can live quite happily without oxygen – indeed, oxygen may even poison them. If they thrive in the water then it's polluted. Usually they give out a nasty pong, so they are a pretty good guide to the existence of pollution.

Fact: Londoners used to call the River Thames the 'Great Stink'. At Westminster, members of parliament had to close their office windows to keep out the smell. Fish kept well away from London. They knew what was good for them! The situation became so bad that 30 years ago a massive attempt was made to clean up the Thames, and in 1974 a salmon swam into London for the first time in 100 years. This was a cause for great celebration. Salmon are very choosy fish and can only live in the cleanest waters.

Oxygen Indicators **

Small fresh-water animals are good pollution indicators. Some species have to live in very clean water whilst others grub out an existence in sewers.

Go pond-dipping with friends and you will collect a lot of important information about the level of oxygen in the water you investigate.

You will need:
a pair of rubber gloves
a pair of wellies
plastic jars with lids and, if possible, handles. The
  lids should have small holes
a pond-dipping net
a hand lens
a clear working space
a wide-ended dropper
a small white tray
a 0-100°C thermometer
a microscope slide

Animals to look out for! See pages 85–6 for full description.

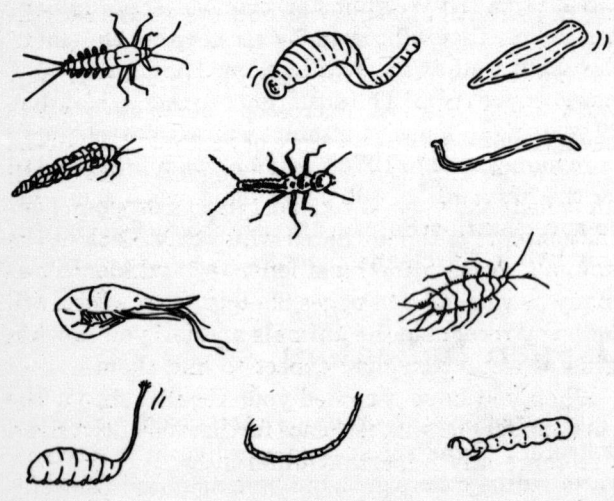

How to go about it

Find a spot by the river bank where you can put your equipment and where there are lots of weeds and algae around the water's edge. Water weeds produce oxygen and are a food source to crustaceans, larval insects and small fish. They are a sign that it is a good place for pond-dipping. Dredge through the small water-plants with your net. Run clear water, away from the plants, through the net to remove any mud. Transfer the contents to the jar and note down a brief description of the place where you take your sample. Include in your description any possible causes of pollution such as sewage works, a power station or a busy road. (See the table overleaf.)

If you do have a thermometer check the temperature of the water. Dip the bulb just below the surface – don't fall in – and leave it there for a few minutes. Remove the thermometer and record the temperature immediately. Is the temperature over 20°C? Then waste heat from industry or power stations may be a cause of pollution.

When your jars are full, take them back to your work space. Place a microscope slide on a white background – a tile or a piece of paper will do. Insert the dropper into the jar and transfer a few small animals to the slide. If you don't have a dropper, pour the contents of the jar into a white tray. Look at the animals through the hand lens. Try and identify as many as you can. On pages 85–6 is a key which will help you recognize the animals and tell you in what kind of water you may expect to find them.

When you have recorded your results, repeat the pond-dipping at another place further along the river. Are there any important differences?

Location	Name of animal	Nos	Temp.	Kind of water (river, stream etc.)	Signs of pollution
Spring river	Fresh water shrimp	2	8c	River	Some floating litter

Indicator animals

Kind of water	Animal	Description
Clean water only	mayfly nymph	About 6mm in length with leafy gills
	stone fly nymph	About 14mm in length
Slightly polluted water	caddis fly larva	About 10mm long
	leech	
	shrimp	Yellow-green, stuck to stones
	flatworm	
	blackfly larva	About 4mm long

Indicator animals

Kind of water	Animal	Description
Very polluted water	bloodworm	Bright red and about 16mm long
	water louse	Grey-brown, about 12mm long found in slow-moving streams amongst weeds
	rat-tailed maggot	Grey, about 10mm long with breathing tube through tail
	sludgeworm	About 50mm long

Trees – Why Do We Need Them

Leaves keep the air fresh by renewing supplies of oxygen.

For paper and fuel.

As shelter for small animals and plants.

Branches protect plants, animals and humans from rain and nasty weather.

Bark is a good food source for woodpeckers, beetles and caterpillars.

Mushrooms and toadstools like dark wet places. Fungi and insects and germs love autumn leaf litter.

OXYGEN PUMPS
WOOD
LEAFY UMBRELLAS
HOLES & PITS
BARK
AN AUTUMN FEAST
THE GREAT TRANSPORT SYSTEM OF THE SOIL

Roots are great suction pumps. They draw up important nutrients from deep down in the soil to the surface.

The Tree That Captured A King's Son

During biblical times, Absalom was at war with his father, King David. Absalom had long flowing hair of which he was very proud, but his hair and a tree proved to be his downfall. As he was riding away from the field of battle, his hair caught in the branches of a tree. He was unable to free himself and was captured and killed.

The Oak That Hid A King

During the English Civil War, King Charles II was on the run after the Battle of Worcester. If the Republicans had captured him it would have changed the course of English history. They didn't. During one of the searches he hid in an oak and only just avoided capture.

Even Trees Need A Spring Clean

Dust is irritating stuff. It has a nasty habit of settling on things. Dust settles in your eyes and gets up your nose. It carries fleas, germs and harmful substances like lead.

Trees suffer from dust pollution more than humans and other animals. We can sweep it all away; trees can't. The dust blocks tiny pores in their leaves and stops them working properly. These pores are called *stomata*. Carbon dioxide gas from the air passes through the *stomata* into the leaves and helps them to produce their own food.

Look at the underside of a leaf through a hand lens and you can see the tiny holes of the *stomata*.

The *stomata* also allow water vapour to escape from their leaves. Trees take up important minerals from the soil by means of a stream of water. This stream moves through the trunk, then out through the *stomata* where the water evaporates. If dust blocks the *stomata* the water cannot escape. The water stream stops moving and the trees cannot use the minerals they need.

The minerals are not only important to the tree. The tree's roots bring the minerals to the surface where they enrich the soil and make extra food for smaller plants.

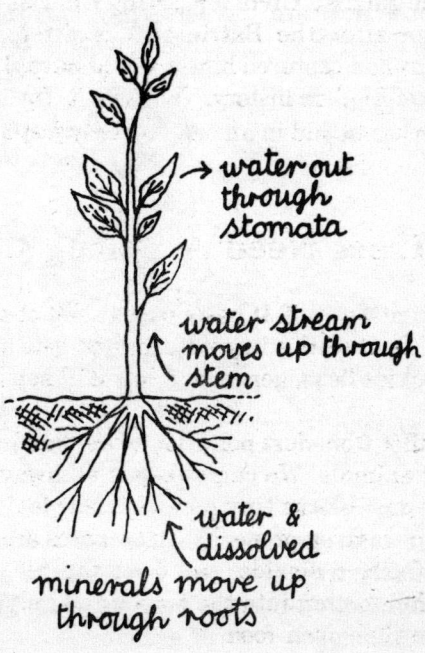

Do The Trees In Your Area Need A Spring Clean? *

You will need
sheets of filter paper
sticky tape
a pair of scissors

What happens
The trees that suffer most from dust are the evergreens because they keep their leaves throughout the year. This means they cannot shed their dusty leaves in the autumn and grow fresh clean ones. The flat-leaved trees, like the oak and the horse chestnut, are luckier. They lose their sooty deposits when the rain falls and washes them away.

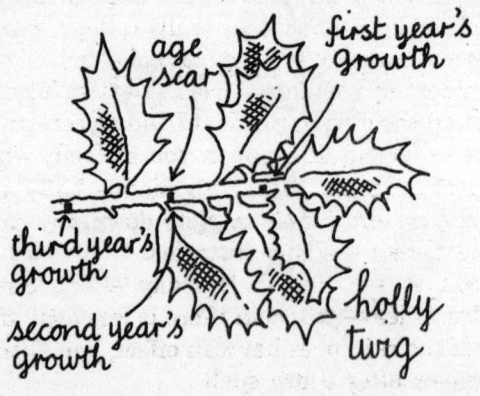

The holly is the best evergreen to test. Remove a twig from a holly tree. How can you find the age of the leaf? Well, holly twigs are very obliging. They leave age scars for each year of growth.

Now that you can record the age of the leaves, it's time to start collecting the dust. Fold the sheet of filter paper in half. Firmly wipe the paper along the leaf twice. Test one leaf for each year.

One half of the paper will contain dust from the upper part of the leaf. This is the greener surface. The other half contains dust from the lower side of the leaf.

Cut around the strips on which you collected the dirt and tape it into your table. Repeat this experiment for a leaf from each year of growth.

Which side of the leaf generally collects more dust? Upper or lower? Which leaves collected most dust? The older or younger leaves? Do two firm wipes collect all the dust on the leaf? Did your results turn out as expected? If not, can you find out why?

Repeat the experiment with another holly tree. See how the results compare. Note down any causes of the dust, like roads or factories.

Check to see if rain has any effect. Sample a number of leaves to see if there is less dust after the rain. If the rain does have an effect, you should test the leaves after a dry spell.

Record your results in a table like this:

	Dust Collected	
Age of Leaf	Upper Leaf	Lower Leaf

Is Traffic A Tree's Worst Enemy? **

Does traffic hurt trees? Exhaust fumes carry a lot of dust. Much of the dust lands on trees which line the roads. People live near roads. If we know what happens to trees, we should have a good idea about whether humans suffer from dust pollution. The next experiment looks at the damage traffic does to trees.

You can explore as many roads as you like but include the following roads at least:

A motorway or A-road with fast-moving heavy traffic.
A main road in a town or city where the traffic moves slowly.
A quiet country or suburban road.

On each road there should be trees planted by the side or within a few hundred yards.

Check the dust on the leaves of a tree as you did in the experiment called 'Do The Trees In Your Area Need A Spring-Clean' see p. 90. Deciduous trees, with their flat broad leaves, are easier to test than evergreens with their small spiky leaves. Check the same species of tree each time. Chestnuts, sycamores and planes are found by most roads.

Wipe three leaves on one of the lower branches of your chosen tree. (Remember the leaves on deciduous trees will be about the same age.) Tape the sheet of filter paper in your notebook. Record the weather conditions. Don't carry out your survey after it has rained. There must be three days of dry weather before you wipe the leaves.

How do you count traffic? Stand at one point and count the vehicles that pass? It is not quite that simple. Heavy lorries emit much more exhaust dust than cars so you will need a grading for each vehicle. The table below grades vehicles as dust-producers.

Type of vehicle	Dust Points
Articulated lorry	6
Coach or bus	5
Light lorry or large van	4
Small coach or minibus	3
Motor car	2
Motor cycle	1

Count the traffic for 15 minutes at each road and record your results in a copy of the table below.

Type of road: (Is it motorway/A-road/busy city/quiet city/suburban/country?)

Time of Day: Between 1pm-2pm Friday

Weather conditions: Sunny and dry

Type of vehicle	numbers	Dust points per vehicle	Total
Articulated lorry	1	6	6
Coach or bus	4	5	20
Light lorry/ larger van	3	4	12
Small coach/ minibus	3	3	9
Motor car	42	2	84
Motor cycle	4	1	4

Grand total 135

Choosing a weekday, carry out one survey during the morning or evening rush hour and another around midday when the traffic is lighter. There's no need to record each survey on the same day. Ask your friends to help you out. Assign each friend to a road, take down your results at the same time and report back. By your results for each road, tape samples of dust collected from leaves of trees by the side of the road. Now you have the evidence that traffic is a dust-spreader.

You might expect the busiest roads to have trees laden with dust. On motorways and similar busy roads the traffic rushes along and creates wind currents. This may prevent the dust settling on trees. With slow-moving traffic the vehicles give off an exhaust with clouds of dust. Exhaust fumes are rich in lead which is harmful to small children. Make a note of any schools in the area.

If you are counting the traffic on a motorway *do not approach the road*. Count the vehicles from a distance, if possible. Take samples of dust from trees in the area but never go up to the verge.

Bird-Loving Trees

Pigeons roost in ledges and nest in church towers. Many birds perch on telegraph wires. They use our technology to their own advantage. Once, in the country, I saw a bird's nest suspended from a beam in a kitchen. The nest was safe because it was high up away from humans, dogs and cats. Other birds didn't see it. The birds had good pickings from the kitchen waste to feed their nestlings.

Trees are still the big favourite for birds. Woodpeckers especially find lots of tasty insects and caterpillars in the bark. And trees are ideal for nesting. All trees improve the appearance of a city but some trees are much better homes for birds than others. The right kind of tree should be planted to attract bird life to the city, so . . .

Do A Bird A Favour **

You will need
a small illustrated guide to trees
a small illustrated guide to birds
notebook
paper
a pair of binoculars
patience!

How to go about it
Carry out this survey during spring, summer and early autumn. Spend about 15 minutes each day studying a particular tree. One day you could watch an oak and the next day gaze at a beech with eagle eyes! Remember you are more likely to see birds like the owl nearer to dusk.

Record the name of any bird that spends more than a few seconds in or near the tree. If you can't recognize the bird at first, note its colouring, size, length of tail and song. Look up the features later in your guide.

Don't stand too near a tree otherwise you'll frighten away the birds. Woods attract plenty of birdlife but the leaf cover makes it difficult to see the individual birds. Try different locations for yourself. It will take

	Oak	Ash	Yew	Larch	Laburnum	Rowan	Sycamore	Plane
Starling								
Blackbird								
Robin								
Crow								
House Sparrow								
Bullfinch								
Magpie								
Swift								
Pigeon								
Black-headed Gull								

time to get accustomed to spotting the birds but after a few days you'll recognize them without the guide.

This project will not only help you identify the right kinds of tree but you may discover birds you have not seen before. Record your sightings with a tick, in a table like the one opposite. I have listed some trees and birds commonly found in a town or city but you can add to the list. You'll need a large sheet of paper and a note-book.

Turn Over A New Leaf **

Autumn – when leaves and tree say goodbye for another year. Mushrooms, toadstools, worms and germs have a whale of a time when trees shed their leaves. They break down and feed off the riches. Some leaves are easy to break down. They release nutrients into the soil and enrich the earth. These leaves *decompose* easily. They readily attract lots of small animals and insects. Decomposition is very important in Nature because it releases materials that were locked up in the leaves.

Which leaves decompose most easily? Those on which fungi and germs have a good feed. Leaves that decompose slowly and with difficulty can be a bit of a nuisance. They cover large areas and prevent other living things from settling there. Easily decomposed leaves are generous. They give up all their goodies without much fuss. Bad decomposers are mean. They lock up lots of useful chemicals and don't give them back to the soil. The only good thing about them is that they are fun to crunch with your feet.

We should discourage the planting of bad decomposers in parks, gardens and leisure areas. In the next project you investigate which trees produce leaves that decompose easily.

You will need
at least 4 large cardboard boxes with small holes in the bottom
a trowel
thin cotton mesh or muslin
drawing-pins
a selection of leaves from different trees

How to go about it
Start your investigation at the beginning of autumn by collecting leaves from a variety of trees. Take fallen leaves but they should still be firm and in one piece. Collect three leaves, of different sizes, from each tree. On the next page you will see pictures of some common leaves which will help to identify them.

Half fill the boxes with earth you find around the leaves. Try to include lots of small soil animals, but avoid snails and slugs. Place the leaves on the surface of the soil. (Each box should contain one kind of leaf only.) Cover the box with muslin by tacking the edges with drawing-pins to the corners of the box. This stops the leaves from blowing away. Leave the box in the garden or another open area.

Note the date when you put the leaves in the box. Check the box daily to see when the leaves have broken down. How can you tell when this has happened? This is the day when you can no longer recognize the leaf. It will have completely disintegrated.

Copy the table on page 100 into your notebook and record what you have measured.

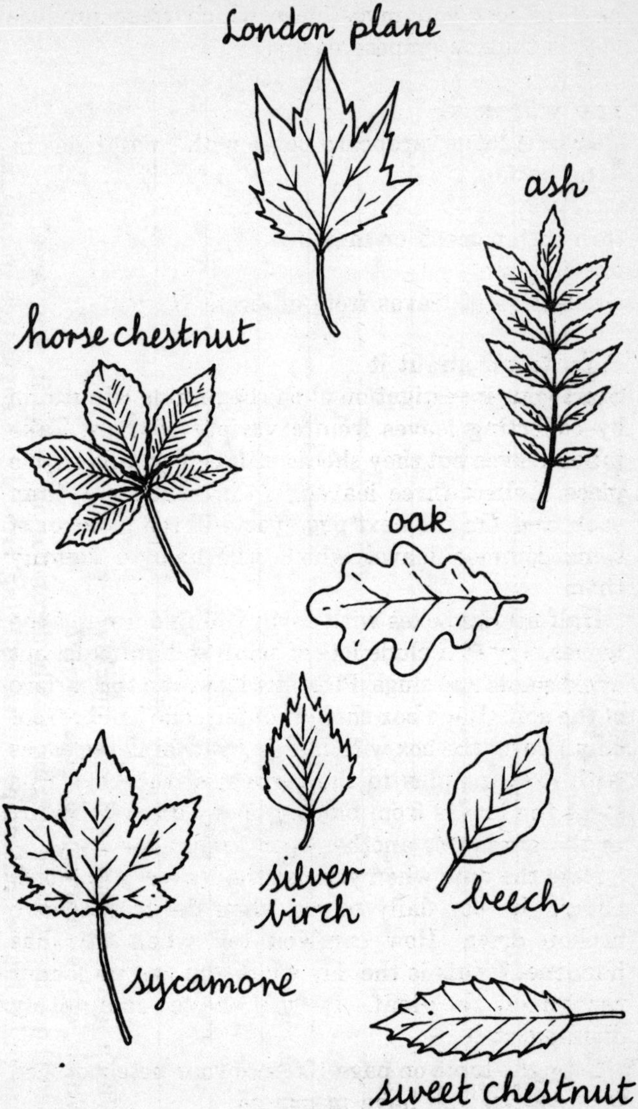

London plane

ash

horse chestnut

oak

sycamore

silver birch

beech

sweet chestnut

99

Leaf	Date leaf put in box	Date leaf decomposed	Days to decompose
Oak			
Ash			
Sycamore			
Plane			
Beech			
Chestnut			

Which leaves decomposed most quickly?
Which leaves decomposed most slowly?
Are there many trees bearing slowly decomposing leaves in your area?
Are there many undecomposed leaves lying around the same tree in autumn?

Where Do Soil Animals Live? **

Trees need small animals to turn over the soil and help break down their leaves. These animals need trees so they can use the leaves for shelter, feed on animals that live on the leaves or feed on the fruit from the trees. You can find out which are the most popular trees with these little beasties. Autumn is the best time to do this project, and you can find out where soil animals live by using pitfall traps.

You will need
small plastic cartons (yogurt cartons are ideal)
a trowel
a hand lens
a white tray
a book on woodland life or insects, see page 127.

How to go about it
Set traps near the bases of different trees. The animals fall into the traps where you can count and identify them. Dig a hole within a few feet of the trunk. The hole should be slightly larger than the carton. Insert the carton into the hole so its top is level with the soil's surface.

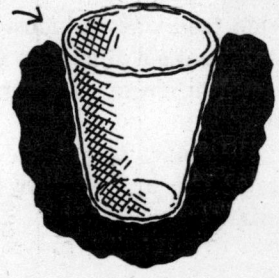

insert carton into hole → so that its top is level with surface of soil

cover wood at entrance with loose soil & leaves

Pack any spaces around the carton with soil and drop in a few leaves to help shelter the animals when they fall in the trap. Cover the top of the carton with a light piece of wood supported by small pebbles and disguise the entrance to the trap with loose soil and dead leaves.

Leave the trap overnight. Next day, tip the contents of the trap into the white tray. Examine the soil animals with your hand lens and see if any animals match up with those on the opposite page.

Count up the number of animals you trap near each tree.
Which tree was the most popular?
Does it make a difference if you carry out this project under different weather conditions, or in another place?
What changes do weather and location make?
What trees are popular both with birds and soil animals?

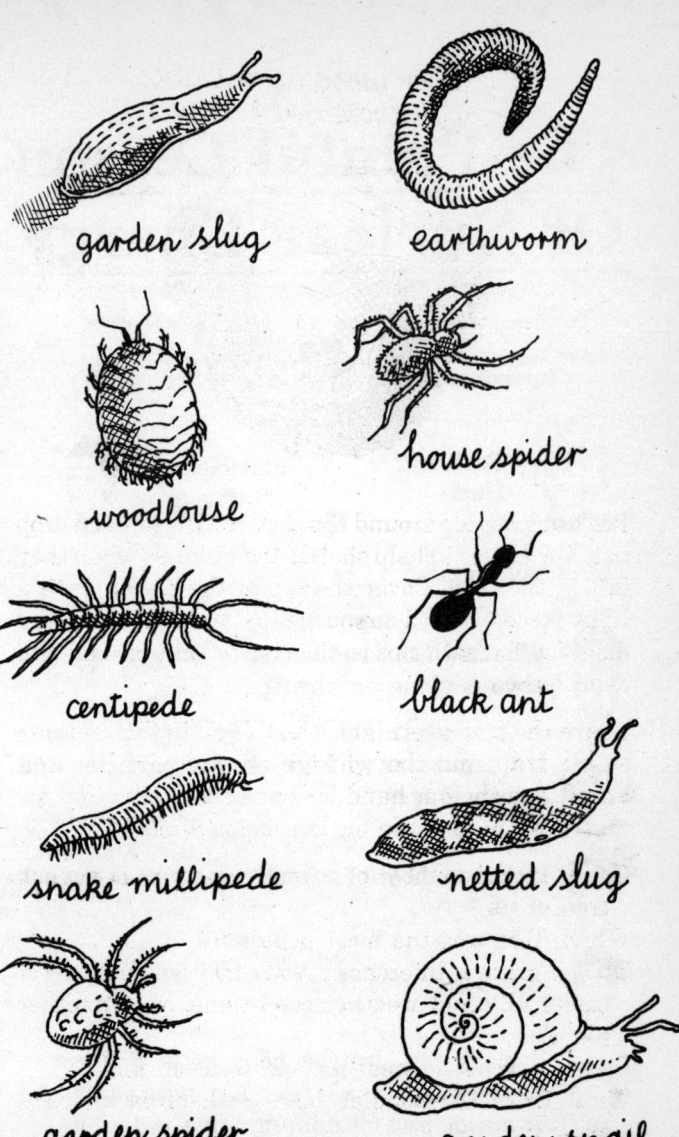

The Painful Lesson
Of Nuclear Energy

.... Introducing Joe

 Professor Nutt   and Holly Twigg

The lesson begins:

 What's all this radioactivity thing people are always going on about?

 It's a mixture of high energy particles and energy waves.

 Unfortunately it's invisible so we can't get out of its way.

 Is it dangerous then?

 Yep. It can destroy body cells and cause diseases like cancer. Certain substances like uranium and plutonium give out a lot of radioactivity. They're very dangerous.

Uranium? I've heard of that. Isn't that the stuff that makes nuclear bombs explode?

Quite correct. Nuclear power stations run on uranium too.

Yeah. So how does it all work?

Well, uranium is made up of tiny atoms. Each uranium atom has a large central part called a nucleus. The nucleus contains really tiny particles. Here is a sketch of an atom:

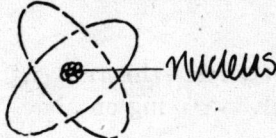

It's a bit like the solar system with the nucleus taking the place of the Sun. Some uranium nuclei are unstable. That means they 'crack up' to release radioactivity.

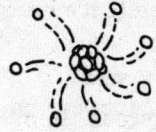

Is uranium radioactive all the time then?

Yes. But we can control the way uranium nuclei crack up.

How can you do that?

We start off a chain reaction. First, we bombard uranium atoms with particles called neutrons. The nucleus actually contains neutrons. When a neutron collides with a uranium nucleus it makes it crack up and release all its energy. This collision releases other neutrons which cause more uranium nuclei to crack up.

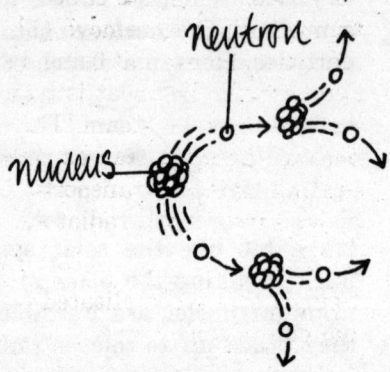

And so it goes on. This chain reaction builds up and produces so much energy that it leads to an explosion. That's what happens with a nuclear bomb.

Are nuclear power-stations like nuclear bombs?

Not quite. In power-stations we control the chain reactions very carefully. We use a material called a moderator to do this. Most power-stations have graphite as a moderator but water can be used too. A bomb does not have a moderator.

How do nuclear power-stations work?

All the nuclear collisions take place in a vessel called a reactor. When the nuclei release lots of energy the reactor becomes very hot. A liquid called a coolant runs through pipes to remove the heat from the reactor and prevent it being damaged through overheating. The heat is transported to boil water and make steam. The coolant carries heat in the same way as water in a central heating system transports heat from the boiler through the radiators.

Sounds like a complicated way of making a big cup of tea?

True. Remember it's a very big kettle and produces energy for lots of people. Anyway, the steam in a nuclear power-station causes a turbine to rotate. In its turn the turbine drives a generator. The generator converts the rotating energy of the turbine into electrical energy. This is distributed as electricity to the National Grid. The system which transports

electric power around the country. Here's a picture of what goes on.

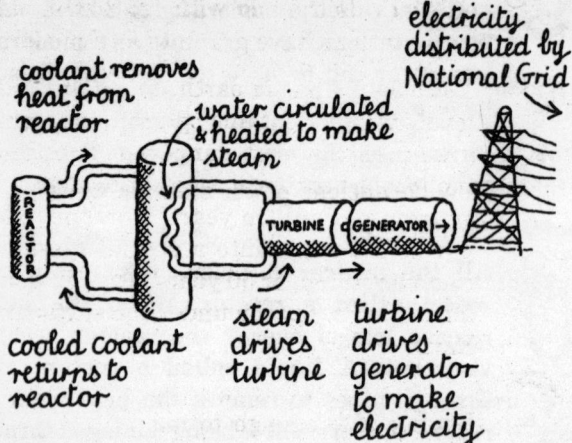

 Sounds great! It doesn't produce all the dirt and muck and oil slicks and all that acid rain pollution you get from coal and oil. Why is everybody making a fuss about nuclear power?

 This is where I come in. First, the uranium wears out. There is a large site in Britain that processes waste fuel so it can be used again. That site is called Sellafield. Sellafield disposes of a lot of nuclear waste. Most of the waste is radioactive. The less dangerous radioactivity is called low-level waste. Until recently, the low-level waste was piped into the Irish Sea. Many people who live on the English west coast and in Ireland were upset because the Irish Sea is the most radioactive stretch of water in the world.

Wow! That's terrible. I wonder how the fish feel about it! If that's the low-level waste what on earth do they do with high-level waste.

 You mean what *in* earth. Much of the high-level waste contains plutonium. This is known as the most dangerous substance in the world because it stays radioactive for a quarter of a million years. Now they plan to inject this waste into a special glass which could be stored for 50 years. Then it would be buried in rocks deep under the surface of the Earth.

 Sounds safe enough to me.

 It *sounds* safe but we don't know if it *is* safe. What might happen if your great-grandchildren accidentally dig up this waste?

 My great-grandchildren! That's looking ahead a bit.

 It may be, but we want to leave the world a pleasant place for future generations. It is such a big problem that some scientists have suggested sending all the waste into outer space.

 Just when I'm thinking nuclear power might be the answer to all our problems you come up with all this stuff. Now it all sounds so dangerous. Is there anything else?

 There sure is. The nuclear waste has to be moved from the power-stations to Sellafield. It's carried on trains in heavy steel flasks. They are supposed to be accident proof but if they did smash . . . well!

 Yeah. I see what you mean. Radioactivity all over the place. What about accidents at nuclear power-stations like Chernobyl?

 That's right. The radioactivity from Chernobyl poisoned millions of acres of rich farmland and blew with winds all over Europe. No one knows how many people would suffer from terrible accidents like that at Chernobyl.

 Phew! What can we do?

 Well, there are two things for starters. Why don't you suggest mounting an exhibition in your school so more people can learn about nuclear power – and its problems. Ask your teacher and the school librarian to help. Ask your friends to cut out any articles that they find in magazines and newspapers. There are many organizations like Friends of the Earth who can supply you with leaflets and other information.

 That's all very well, but what can we *do*?

110

 It is important that everyone knows about the benefits and dangers of nuclear power. There is definite action we can all take. There are plans to build more nuclear power-stations. This is to meet extra energy demands in the next few years. If we used less energy we would need less electricity. We would save money and there would be no need for extra power-stations. So, the motto is . . .

SAVE ENERGY AND SAVE LIFES

Tick the boxes that best answer the questions. Are you an energy saver? Find out, then try out the questions on your friends.

1 How often do you have lights on that you don't need?

A Never ☐   B Once or twice weekly ☐

C Frequently ☐

2 Is your storage heater well lagged to keep in heat energy? (To answer 'Yes' the lagging should be firm and there should be no spaces for the heat to escape.)

A Yes ☐   B No ☐

3 Do you re-cycle waste like glass and vegetables?

A Yes ☐   B No ☐

4 Do you put lids on saucepans when cooking?
   A Yes ☐   B No ☐

5 What do you like best?
   A Whole boiled potatoes ☐
   B Mashed potatoes ☐
   C Fried potatoes ☐
   D Chips ☐

6 When you boil water for a cup of tea, how much water is left in the kettle after you have poured the tea?
   A None ☐   B A little ☐   C Lots ☐

7 Open the door of your refrigerator. Is it
   A Empty? ☐
   B Half empty? ☐
   C Full or nearly full? ☐

8 Tear off a thin strip of paper. Close the door of the refrigerator on it. Can you now remove the paper easily?
   A Yes ☐   B No ☐

9 Go and check all the hot water taps in your home. How many are dripping?
   A More than one ☐   B One ☐   C None ☐

10 Do you usually
   A Bath? ☐   B Shower? ☐

11 What lighting do you have in your kitchen?
A Fluorescent tubes ☐
B Light bulbs ☐

Answers and points

1. A=3; B=1; C=0
2. A=2; B=0
3. A=2; B=0
4. A=2; B=0
5. A=2; B=2; C=0; D=1
   Finely chopped food cooks more quickly.
6. A=0 (Careful! You'll boil the kettle dry!); B=1; C=0
7. A=0 (wasteful!); B=1; C=3
8. A=0; B=1
9. A=0; B=0; C=2
10. A=0; B=2
    Showers use less hot water than baths and keep you just as clean and warm
11. A=1; B=0

What's your energy rating?

18 to 21 - Wonderful! Who needs nuclear power-stations?

15 to 17 - Good. But there's still more energy to be saved.

10 to 14 - All your pocket money down the energy drain.

1 to 9 - You need a power-station of your own.

0 - HELP!

 The most important thing we can do is help to develop other energy sources which are a lot safer. Almost all our energy needs come from fossil fuels and nuclear power. Fossil fuels are coal, oil and gas. But we're going to run out of these sources of energy. It's like a race. Coal, oil and gas and uranium are the front-runners but they're getting tired.

 Who's catching up?

 There's energy from hot rocks!

It's called geothermal energy. Under ground there are hot volcanic rocks whose heat can provide hot water. Next, rushing up to the front, is wind energy. The energy from howling winds can operate wind generators that produce electricity. Certain areas like the Orkneys and the fens are windy and would be ideal as a site for wind generators. About 20 per cent of our electricity could come from wind energy – and we're not likely to run out of it. Problem is . . .

... We never know when it'll blow.

Then there's the sea. We can convert the motion of the waves into electricity. As long as there's a sea we'll have waves, so its worth tapping this energy source. It would be very useful for small islands with small populations.

And what about hilly areas with rivers? Yes. Hydro-electricity is ideal for these areas. Water falls on to a turbine from a great height. The turbine drives a generator which produces electricity.

And finally . . . HERE COMES THE SUN!

Fact: More energy comes from the Sun to the Earth in a single day than the whole world uses in a year.

Fact: Even the cloudy countries of the North could use it. The total solar energy falling on these lands in one year is more than one hundred times greater than all the energy they need!

Fact: People living in warm countries have their water heated through special solar panels. They absorb the heat from the Sun.

Fact: Tens of millions of solar-powered watches and calculators are sold each year.

Fact: The Sun should burn brightly for another few billion years. We're not going to run out of solar energy just yet!

Why don't we use solar energy all the time?

Because we would have to trap the sunlight in great parabolic reflectors. They take up an enormous amount of space.

Fact: If Britain produced all its energy directly from the Sun we couldn't live here. The entire island would be covered by great reflectors!

Fact File

LEAD

Why is it dangerous?
It's a poison. Lead damages the nervous system. Very young children suffer from lead poisoning because their brains have not developed fully.

How does lead enter the body?
In almost every way possible. If you breathe, eat or drink you're liable to take in lead.

Breathing   Breathe in petrol fumes on a busy road and you're inviting gases containing lead inside your body.

Eating   Where have your vegetables come from? Lead in the air falls on to vegetables and contaminates them. Make sure you wash them carefully.

Drinking   Old water pipes are made of lead. Water that runs through the pipes dissolves the lead. It may appear in the tap-water. Find out what your water pipes are made of. Take particular care of hot water from the storage tank. You should never drink water from the hot tap. Watch out for food cans. Some contain solder which is a metal alloy made from lead and tin. Fruit juices in cans dissolve lead.

Why can't our bodies get rid of lead?

They don't know how to. Lead doesn't occur naturally in the human body. We have no use for it.

What is lead used for?

It is an 'anti-knock' device in petrol. This means it makes the petrol burn evenly.

Old water pipes.

Solder in canned foods.

Old pewter mugs. Those made recently are perfectly safe. Be very careful of any 'glazed' pottery. It may contain lead.

An ingredient in cosmetics.

Car batteries.

Fishing weights. Careless fishermen leave them in the water. Weights kill swans when swallowed by mistake.

Where is lead most dangerous?
On roads with slow-moving traffic. When stationary cars have their engines running they produce plumes of lead-carrying exhaust gas.

What can we do?
Avoid roads with lots of busy traffic.

Don't drink water from the hot water tap.

Eat plenty of dairy products and fruit, particularly apples and bananas. These foods contain calcium, phosphates, magnesium and iron. They are minerals that control any damage caused by the lead.

Find out if there are any infant or nursery schools on main roads. Write a letter to the Environmental Health department of your local council. Ask them if they have checked the lead levels in the area of the school. If you live on a main road find out if the levels of lead in the air around you exceeds the legal limit. If you're not happy with a reply from the council, the Friends of the Earth will help. See the appendix on page 125 for their addresses.

Action!

When you have completed some of the projects in this book you may have discovered that your environment needs a spring-clean. Don't sweep it up all on your own! Get together a group of friends and form a pressure group. If you want to join a group find out from your local library if there are any local environmental groups. Whether you're in a group or not, the following addresses will prove useful.

> Royal Society of Nature Conservation,
> WATCH,
> The Green,
> Nettleham,
> Lincoln LN2 2NR
> Telephone: (0522) 752326

This is a national club for young people who care about wildlife and their environment. WATCH will give you the address of a group in your area if you send an SAE. They also supply the Acid Drops kit. Members receive a magazine called 'Watchword' which tells you about national projects and lots of fun things you can do.

> London Wildlife Trust,
> 80 York Way,
> London N1 9AG
> Telephone: (01) 278 6612

This organization aims to protect wildlife that, like us, inhabit the city. This includes wild plants and animals like foxes, hedgehogs and owls. The LWT run nature reserves and produce leaflets that tell you how you can protect birds and mammals. London Wildlife Trust also sells fun stickers and badges about conservation. They can tell you about similar groups in other large cities.

> English Heritage,
> (Historic Buildings and Monuments Commission),
> 1–17 Great Marlborough Street,
> London W1V 1AF
> Telephone: (01) 734 6010

'Keep' is for young people interested in preserving historic buildings. It organizes projects and events. Write with an SAE.

> Seed Bank and Exchange,
> 44, Albion Road,
> Sutton,
> Surrey SM2 5TF

Are there any derelict sites near you? Do you have bare patches in unpromising areas of your garden? They may be growing wild flowers already but you could spruce them up by planting attractive wild flowers of your own. You must be careful, though. Some flowers spread like weeds and can damage other plants. Seed Bank and Exchange publish catalogues and sell seeds. They can advise you where and how to plant. Write to them for information with your address and enclose two second-class stamps.

Getting Together

Ask your friends if they are interested in changing things in your neighbourhood. Pin up cards or posters in your school library or on a school notice-board, with your name and address, so other interested young people can contact you. It's a good idea to specify the age range of your group. A picture on a poster will draw attention to it.

When you have all gathered together as a group arrange a time and place for your next meeting. At this meeting the members should form a committee and appoint four officers:

A chair person He or she will chair the meeting and make sure that those of you who have something to say get a chance to speak. During the meeting members indicate to the chair person that they want to air their views.

A secretary The secretary writes away for information and deals with all correspondence. He or she usually takes notes and keeps a record of what is said at the meeting and informs members of events or meetings.

A treasurer The treasurer collects subscriptions, keeps an account of the money available and makes sure there is enough money to carry out projects.

A publicity person He or she will be responsible for publicity and organize your campaigns.

You need not have just one person for each post. People can rotate or share a position. You can elect more people to take on different jobs as and when the need arises.

The committee should agree on an agenda for each meeting. Suppose you are going to investigate the effect of Acid Rain in your area. At the meeting you will have to decide:

What ponds, rivers, streams, lakes, canals you are going to investigate.
Who is going to do the testing
When you are going to do the testing
Where you are going to get the equipment
Who sends away for pH indicators
How you can publicize the results, if necessary
What groups can help you
What funds you need for the project
When you report back

Remember, meetings have to be organized, so

1 make sure everyone knows the date, time and place of the next meeting.
2 make sure you have a supply of pens, pencils and paper.
3 make sure the secretary brings along all correspondence.
4 make sure you have a list of topics to discuss and suggestions of possible activities.
5 make sure everyone can sit comfortably. People lose patience if they have to stand or sit in uncomfortable positions.

Do's And Don'ts

DO try and make people interested in what you're doing.
DO contact any organizations that can help you
DO publicize your investigations through local papers, libraries, schools and youth clubs.

DON'T try to change things all on your own. For example, you must not clear a pond which is not your own without letting the local authorities know. Organizations like Friends of the Earth and BTCV can advise you.

DON'T keep the results of your investigations to yourself. Doing projects with friends is more fun, more exciting and worthwhile.

Organizations For The Group

Friends of the Earth,
377 City Road,
London EC1V 1NA
Telephone: (01) 837 0731

This organization campaigns about damage to our environment. It draws attention to matters such as wildlife, acid rain, pollution, transport and nuclear power. They can tell you where to get the information you need.

British Trust for Conservation Volunteers (BTCV),
36 St. Mary's Street,
Wallingford,
Oxfordshire OX10 0EU
Telephone: (0491) 39766

BTCV can advise you on projects like clearing derelict sites, digging ponds and planting trees. They print information sheets and give practical advice. BTCV work mainly with schools and youth clubs. If you do have a good idea about a local project on conservation tell your teacher about BTCV. The main centre will tell your teacher who to contact.

Keep Britain Tidy Group,
Bostel House,
37 West Street,
Brighton BN1 2RE
Telephone: (0273) 23585

This group aims to improve our surroundings by controlling litter. Litterbugs are banned. If litter is a big problem in your area and you want to organize a clean-up campaign, then write and ask them for advice. They produce leaflets, booklets and activity packs.

Kodak Conservation Awards,
5-11 Theobalds Road,
London WC1X 8SH
Telephone: (01) 405 8979

They help young people to take action to improve their neighbourhood by awarding funds. If you have good ideas for conservation, even in a very small way, ask them for information and how to apply for an award.

The organizations below are specialized and may interest you:

The Cat Survival Trust,
Marlind Centre,
Codicote Road,
Welwyn,
Herts. AL6 9TU
Telephone: (043871) 6873

They work to conserve smaller and less well-known species of wildcat. They produce a journal.
Membership: £3 junior – under 16.

The Otter Trust,
Earsham,
Nr Bungay,
Suffolk NR35 2AF
Telephone: (0986) 3470

They help to conserve otters. Junior members receive a magazine. There is an open day with games and quizzes for young members each year.
Membership: £4 junior.

World Wildlife Fund,
Panda House,
11-13 Ockford Road,
Godalming,
Surrey GU7 1QU
Telephone: (04868) 20551

They support threatened species throughout the world. Junior members receive a youth magazine.
Membership: £3 junior.

Young Ornithologists' Club,
R.S.P.B.,
The Lodge,
Sandy,
Beds. SG19 2DL
Telephone: (0767) 80551

They run birdwatching activities for young people. There are lots of exciting projects and competitions for members.
Membership: £3.25; Family membership: £4

Junior Herps,
80 Curzon Avenue,
Enfield,
Middx. EN3 4UU
Telephone: (01) 805 0745

They run activities for young people interested in reptiles and amphibians. That includes animals like snakes, turtles, tortoises, frogs, toads and newts. There is a junior newsletter and bulletin.
Membership: £3 ages 9-17.

BOOKS

Usborne publish a number of very useful 'Spotters' Guides' which help you to spot lots of different plants and animals and tell you a lot of interesting things to do besides. The titles you should particularly look out for are:

Wild Flowers   *Trees*   *Birds*
Woodland Life   *Ponds & Lakes*   *Insects*
Town & City Life

Frederick Warne publish a series of books called the Observer books that help you to identify animals and plants. They are:

Birds   *Trees*   *Lichens*
Pond Life *Wild Flowers*

The British Museum (Natural History) publish a poster called 'Lichens and Air Pollution' which will help you to find out lots more about lichens and what types grow in polluted areas.